AIR CAMPAIGN

JAPAN 1944–45

LeMay's B-29 strategic bombing campaign

MARK LARDAS | ILLUSTRATED BY PAUL WRIGHT

OSPREY PUBLISHING
Bloomsbury Publishing Plc
PO Box 883, Oxford, OX1 9PL, UK
1385 Broadway, 5th Floor, New York, NY 10018, USA
E-mail: info@ospreypublishing.com
www.ospreypublishing.com

OSPREY is a trademark of Osprey Publishing Ltd

First published in Great Britain in 2019

A catalog record for this book is available from the British Library.

ISBN: PB 9781472832467; eBook 9781472832474;
ePDF 9781472832481; XML 9781472832498

19 20 21 22 23   10 9 8 7 6 5 4 3 2 1

Maps by Bounford.com
3D BEVs by Paul Kime
Diagrams by Adam Tooby
Index by Alan Rutter
Typeset by PDQ Digital Media Solutions, Bungay, UK
Printed in Hong Kong through World Print Ltd

Artist's note

Readers may care to note that the original paintings from which the color plates in this book
were prepared are available for private sale. All reproduction copyright whatsoever is retained
by the Publishers. All inquiries should be addressed to: p.wright1@btinternet.com
The Publishers regret that they can enter into no correspondence upon this matter.

Osprey Publishing supports the Woodland Trust, the UK's leading woodland conservation
charity.

To find out more about our authors and books visit www.ospreypublishing.com. Here
you will find extracts, author interviews, details of forthcoming events and the option to
sign up for our newsletter.

Author's Note

The following abbreviations indicate the
sources of the illustrations used in this
volume:
AC – Author's Collection
LOC – Library of Congress,
Washington DC
NARA – National Archives
NMUSAF – National Museum of the
United States Air Force
PASM – Pima Air and Space Museum
PSAM – Palm Springs Air Museum
USAAF – United States Army Air Force
USNHHC – United States Navy
Heritage and History Command

Author's acknowledgments
I would like to thank Greg Kenny the
Education/Program Coordinator of
the Palm Springs Air Museum in Palm
Springs, California and James Stemm,
Director of Collections and Aircraft
Restoration at the Pima Air & Space
Museum in Tucson, Arizona for their
help in preparing this book, and their
patience with my questions. I encourage
readers near these two cities to visit their
museums if you can.

Author's Dedication
For Janet, my late wife. Forty years, eight
months, and three days. Too short. Far
too short.

CONTENTS

INTRODUCTION

The bomber will always get through. So claimed Stanley Baldwin, then Lord President of the Council of Great Britain (and soon to be Prime Minister), in November 1932. It was a principle developed 11 years earlier by Italian General Giulio Douhet in his book *Il dominio dell'aria* (*The Command of the Air*). He predicted that armies and navies were obsolete. Aircraft could overfly them and attack and destroy a nation's vital centers – governmental centers, industry, and transportation networks. Victory would follow the enemies' collapse once these vitals were destroyed.

Douhet's doctrine was soon adopted by air power visionaries around the world. Over the two decades following publication of Douhet's books, air-power advocates in many nations insisted wars could be won through air power alone – through strategic bombing.

Yet between 1921 and 1944 no nation could claim to have achieved Douhet's goal of victory through strategic air power. Nazi Germany claimed it used air power to win the Spanish Civil War and gain victory in the opening days of World War II. Yet Guernica and Rotterdam proved to be less examples of strategic bombing than aerial terrorism linked to ground campaigns. The Luftwaffe's attempts to batter Britain into submission during the Battle of Britain in 1940 and the Blitz of 1940–41 ended in failure. The bomber did not always get through. Nor did civilian morale collapse, as Douhet had predicted'.

Britain's Royal Air Force went even further in its attempt to defeat Germany through strategic bombardment. Britain built thousands of heavy bombers, committing them to a years-long night bombing campaign against the German heartland. Despite 1,000-plane raids and firestorm-generating incendiary raids, by 1944 it was apparent this campaign had failed to force German surrender, even with United States cooperation through daylight bombardment.

No nation was more invested in strategic bombardment than the United States, however. It first flew the B-17, its first monoplane, metal, four-engine bomber, in 1935, four years before the RAF flew its counterpart, the Short Stirling. The B-17 was the United States' first operational heavy bomber when World War II started. It was soon joined by the B-24

Liberator. Over the course of the war a combined total of over 30,000 of these two heavy bombers were built.

Great Britain and Germany pinned their strategic bombing campaigns on area bombardment – the destruction of whole cities. US air-power advocates believed the solution lay in precision bombardment. Highly accurate targeting would place bombs on high-value enemy targets. Knock these out and the enemy would collapse. Better still, bombs would land only on targets of military value. Civilians (except those working in facilities associated with the military, such as aircraft factories) would be spared.

It was a classic American solution: high-tech, delivering a knockout blow which avoided the mass slaughter of trench warfare, and which punished only the guilty – the evildoers actually prosecuting the war. As in a Western, only the bad guys got hurt.

In theory it should work, but reality demonstrated differently, especially in Europe against Germany. Unescorted daylight bombers proved incapable of "getting through" against Nazi air defenses without taking unacceptable losses. Weather frequently obscured targets (preventing accurate bombing), when it did not simply prevent aircraft from flying. There were factories which could have crippled Germany had they been knocked out. (Only two facilities produced tetraethyl-lead, critical to producing high-octane fuel.) US mission planners were either unaware of these choke points or (as with ball bearings) production could be dispersed, preventing knockout precision bombing.

The United States Army Air Corps (which became the Army Air Force in June 1941) remained fully invested in the doctrine of precision daylight strategic bombing even as the failures of strategic bombardment in Europe became apparent. In 1940 it requested development of a new super-bomber; a next generation very heavy bomber which could fly transcontinental distances at unprecedented altitudes and speeds, carrying a bomb load far beyond that which could be carried by either the B-17 or B-24.

Four companies submitted designs. Two aircraft were developed: the Boeing B-29 and the Consolidated B-32. Both had a combat range of 3,200 miles (50 percent greater than the B-24's), and a cruise speed of 290mph (the maximum speed of a B-24). Both could carry in excess of 20,000lb of bombs internally. Both had four 2,200hp 18-cylinder radial engines.

The B-32 was evolutionary. It was a larger, faster version of the B-24, optimized for operations between 10,000 and 20,000ft.

An early-model B-17 in pre-war colors. The B-17 Flying Fortress was the first four-engine monoplane metal bomber fielded by any nation's air force. (AC)

A less ambitious design than the B-29, the Consolidated B-32 Dominator was Boeing's main competitor in the Army Air Corps' very heavy bomber competition. Ordered as a back-up to the B-29, it had a more troubled development than the Superfortress. (AC)

The B-29 was revolutionary. It was intended to operate at 30,000ft. It had a pressurized crew compartment allowing the crew to fly in shirtsleeve conditions. Four turrets, two on top and two below the bomber, were remote-controlled, with computerized targeting. Only the tail guns were manned. To simplify pressurization, the aircraft had a cylindrical cross section and an ovaloid nose, with no break for the windshield. Boeing named it the Superfortress.

With its new super-bomber under development, the Army Air Corps believed it had the bomber to achieve Douhet's dream. Its range was so great that from the beginning the Army Air Force viewed it as a purely strategic asset. The B-29s would be organized into an air force independent of theater commanders, reporting directly to Army Air Force headquarters in Washington DC.

The B-29 first flew in September 1942. By then, the Army Air Force had decided to commit the B-29, with its extremely long range, exclusively against Japan. Its standard heavy bombers had enough range and payload to knock Germany out of the war without the B-29. The B-29 was to be the tool used to show air power alone could knock out an industrial nation.

Japan seemed perfect for a demonstration of air power. It was an island nation. Reaching it with ground troops would require invasion. It was a major industrial nation, with the second largest economy of the Axis nations. Fighting Japanese soldiers was always bloody. Its soldiers fought tenaciously, willing to die as long as they killed some of the enemy doing so. Allied planners wished to avoid the unprecedented bloodshed promised by invading Japan. An air-power victory might also be bloody, but most of the dead would be Japanese, not Allied airmen, sailors, and soldiers.

Using the B-29 depended on actually having the B-29. It was pushed into production at four different factories in four different states almost as soon as the prototype flew. Dispersed production and its novel design (using engines and avionics at the leading edge of aviation technology for its time) meant the bomber's early months were troubled. The engines overheated. A prototype crashed and burned after an engine caught fire during a test flight, killing all aboard and many in the building it hit.

The design changed to incorporate lessons from the flight testing. Due to many changes mandated during development, factories were introducing errors during assembly. In March 1944 each B-29 off the assembly line needed 54 major modifications before being deemed operational. Many early B-29s went straight to maintenance depots for rebuilds to the current standard.

The B-29 was slated to begin combat operations in April 1944. On March 9 General Henry "Hap" Arnold, chief of the Army Air Force, ordered the bombers overseas.

He was told none were available. This was due to teething problems typically encountered in developing a new aircraft. There had been so many revisions to the B-29's design the mechanics could not keep up. (The less-ambitious B-32, which first flew two weeks before the first B-29 flight, experienced even more developmental difficulties than the B-29. Ordered as a backup in case the B-29 failed, it was even further from operational deployment than the troubled B-29.)

The result became known as the Battle of Kansas; an all-out effort to bring the B-29 to operational status. Arnold ordered over 600 mechanics to Salina, Kansas to fix the bombers. By March 26, the bombers started flying overseas. By April 15, 32 B-29s were in India, getting ready to fly to China, from where they could strike Japan.

It would take another two months before B-29s would bomb Japan from Chinese airfields. The airfields were still being built. Bombs, fuel, personnel, and spare parts had to travel over 12,500 miles to reach Chinese airfields. By mid-1944, the Superfortress was operational, launching strikes against Japan. By November, B-29s were attacking Japan from bases in the Marianas Islands, captured in June and July 1944. Those bases were easier to supply, being only 5,700 miles from the US mainland, and were secure from Japanese ground attack. Yet over its first nine months, the aircraft achieved surprisingly little.

Some of this was due to development issues. More was due to operational issues. Initially Superfortresses operated from primitive bases in China, wearing out planes ferrying fuel. Even after new bases in the Marianas Islands opened, results remained disappointing.

Enormous resources had been poured into the Superfortress. In two short years, the B-29 had gone from a concept to a production aircraft. Given the new technology invested in it, simply getting it operational was a significant achievement. It was the most expensive weapon developed during World War II. More was spent developing the B-29 than was spent on the Manhattan Project (which created the atomic bomb). But as the first two months of 1945 ended, a meaningful return on the investment proved elusive. The bombers were not delivering on their promise.

What made this even more frustrating was that the problem was the ineffectiveness of the bombing. Japanese home defenses proved formidable, but not insurmountable. Japan lacked a truly integrated national air defense system. The B-29s were too fast and flew too high to face serious fighter opposition, and they flew above Japanese antiaircraft artillery. Operations and maintenance, getting to Japan without the aircraft crashing en route or back and bombing effectively, proved more difficult obstacles than the Japanese.

With its cigar-cylinder fuselage, long wing, and soaring tail, the B-29 had an elegant appearance to match its formidable performance. This early version of the Superfortress is at an airbase in the United States. (NMUSAF)

Post-mission photograph of Osaka showing incendiary raid damage. Destruction is almost total. Only reinforced concrete buildings remain; even those are burned-out shells. (AC)

It looked like the only way to subdue Japan – despite the promises of America's air-power advocates – was a costly and bloody ground invasion of the home islands.

In January 1945 a new commander took over. Curtis LeMay, one of the Army Air Force's foremost proponents of strategic bombardment, took charge of operations against Japan. He developed new strategies, including supporting a controversial (to the Army Air Force) campaign to interdict Japan's maritime traffic by aerial dropping of mines in Japanese seaways and ports. More controversially, he substituted low-level nighttime incendiary attacks for the high-altitude precision bombing beloved by the Army Air Force. He sent his bombers in at between 5,000 and 10,000ft, ordered most ammunition for the defensive machine guns to be taken off the Superfortresses and sent them against Japan.

After two weeks the verdict was in. Four major Japanese cities were in ruins. Five raids did as much damage as the entire B-29 bombing campaign preceding those attacks. Over the next six months, by combining more fire raids with daylight precision bombardment and naval mines dropped by B-29s, LeMay eviscerated Japan's war-making capability and left its population starving.

His command achieved something no other air force had accomplished previously or would manage afterwards. He forced the surrender of a major military power without the need to commit ground forces. The atomic bombs dropped on Hiroshima and Nagasaki led to the Japanese surrender, but in reality they offered an excuse for the Japanese to acknowledge a reality which already existed. They were already beaten by the B-29 Superfortress.

This is the story of that campaign.

CHRONOLOGY

1921
General Giulio Douhet writes *Il dominio dell'aria* (*The Command of the Air*).

1939
January Boeing begins design of its Model 333, a four-engine bomber design that leads to development of the B-29.

December 2 The War Department invites proposals for a very long-range heavy "super-bomber."

1940
May 11 Boeing submits Model 345 design to the Army Air Corps in response to the super-bomber proposal.

June The Army Air Corps requests a design for a super-heavy bomber from Consolidated as a backup in case the Boeing design fails.

September 6 The Army Air Corps signs contracts with Boeing to produce the B-29 Superfortress and Consolidated to produce the B-32 Dominator.

1941
December 7 Japan attacks Pearl Harbor, bringing the United States into World War II.

1942
September 21 First flight of the prototype B-29.

1944
March Japan reorganizes its home air defense to defend against expected B-29 attacks.

June Imperial Japanese Navy successfully defeats an attempt to create joint Army–Navy air defense of Japan.

June 5 First combat mission flown by B-29s in raid on Bangkok.

June 15 Saipan invaded by United States forces.

June 15–16 First combat B-29 mission flown against Japan. Imperial Iron and Steel Works at Yawata is bombed by China-based 58th Bombardment Wing B-29s.

July 21 Guam invaded by United States forces.

July 24 Tinian invaded by United States forces.

October 12 First B-29s arrive at Isley Field in Saipan.

October 28 First combat mission flown by Marianas-based B-29s, with 18 73rd Bombardment Wing Superfortresses attacking Truk.

November 10 Harmon Field in Guam operational and open to B-29s.

November 10 First 313th Bombardment Wing aircraft begin arriving at Guam.

November 24 First B-29 mission against Japan launched from the Marianas. Tokyo bombed by 111 B-29s from Saipan.

December 27 North Field in Tinian operational, B-29s arrive.

1945
January 10 First 314th Bombardment Wing aircraft begin arriving at Tinian.

January 21 Brigadier General Curtis LeMay relieves Heywood Hansell of command of the B-29s in the Marianas.

B-29 *Incendiary Journey* was photographed from another B-29 during the June 1, 1945 Osaka raid. Damage to its inboard starboard engine from an engine fire and oil leak stains both the wing and horizontal stabilizer. (NMUSAF)

Downtown Osaka prior to World War II. The city was filled with modern office buildings and tree-lined streets. (AC)

January 21 313th Bombardment Wing begins combat operations.

February 4 Experimental incendiary raid on Japanese city of Kobe fails due to small number of bombers and high altitude.

February 19 US Marines invade Iwo Jima.

February 25 314th Bombardment Wing begins combat operations.

March 4 First B-29 makes an emergency landing at Iwo Jima.

March 9–10 First mass incendiary raid on Toyko. Over 267,000 buildings burned and over 83,000 killed.

March 9–18 Five major incendiary raids launched in a 10-day period. Toyko, Nagoya, Kobe, and Osaka attacked.

March 16 Central Field on Iwo Jima operational.

March 24 Precision bombing attacks resume after XXI Bomber Command exhausts stores of incendiary bombs.

March 27 313th Bomb Wing begins mining operations in the Shimonoseki Strait to open Operation *Starvation*.

March 31–April 1 A precision night raid against the Nakajima Musashi aircraft plant in Nagoya is attempted, but fails.

April 1 Okinawa invaded by United States forces. Campaign lasts until June 22.

April 6 Kadena airfield on Okinawa opens and is available as an emergency landing field for B-29s.

April 7 First fighter escort for a B-29 mission, as P-51s escort a daylight mission to bomb the Nakajima aircraft factory at Tokyo. B-29 jamming of Japanese fire control radars employed for the first time.

April 13–16 Second round of incendiary attacks, Tokyo and Tokyo area (Kawasaki) targeted.

April 16–May 10 B-29s begin campaign against Kyushu airfields. Strategic bombing largely suspended to bomb airfields in support of the Okinawa invasion.

May 5 58th Bombardment Wing flies first combat mission from Marianas.

Two members of the crew of this B-29 are thanking the artist (a Seabee), who painted an emblem for the bomber and decorated the plane with caricatures of its crew. (USNHHC)

May 11 Final Kyushu airfield strike flown. Strategic bombing resumes with a daylight raid on an aircraft factory at Kobe.

May 14 Incendiary bombing of Japan's largest cities resumes with a daytime area raid against Nagoya. Between May 14 and June 10 six of Japan's 10 largest cities are burned out in multi-wing, maximum-effort raids.

June 17 Incendiary attacks on Japan's secondary cities begin. They continue until the end of the war.

June 26 315th Bombardment Wing conducts first combat mission.

August 1 Most B-29s sent on combat missions against Japan in a single day. Of 836 B-29s launched, 784 hit targets in Japan.

August 6 *Enola Gay* drops an atomic bomb on Hiroshima.

August 8 The Soviet Union declares war on Japan.

August 9 *Bockscar* drops an atomic bomb on Nagasaki.

August 14 Railyards at Marifu bombed, opening campaign against Japan's transportation system. Last day of offensive combat operations by strategic B-29 bombers.

August 15 Japan surrenders.

August 16 B-29 production ceases with 3,970 production aircraft completed. Aircraft on assembly lines are scrapped in place.

1953
July 27 Last combat mission flown by a B-29 (an armed reconnaissance mission during the Korean War).

1960
June 21 B-29 retired from the USAF inventory.

ATTACKER'S CAPABILITIES
To command the air over Japan

A B-29 begins its take-off run from an airfield in the Pacific. Without the B-29, the subsequent strategic bombing campaign against Japan could not have begun until May 1945, seven months after the first daylight raid on Tokyo. (NMUSAF)

The strategic bombing of Japan was the most ambitious air campaign of World War II. Simply attacking Japan was a challenge. In January 1944 only one production aircraft could carry a significant bomb load 1,600 miles: the notionally operational B-29. But no Allied-controlled airfields even existed within 1,600 miles of Japan's Home Islands. The only Allied-controlled territory within that range of Japan was in China, half the world away from the Continental United States.

Before the United States could begin the campaign, it needed to take Japanese-controlled territory from which B-29s could reach Japan, and build airbases on that territory. It also needed to develop the logistics infrastructure to provide the bases and bombers used in the campaign with necessary fuel, food, weapons, and supplies.

Between January and November 1944 the United States created the capability to launch its strategic bombing campaign. The United States was able to strike Japan as early as June 1944. Its full capabilities would not be in place until April 1945, but it built enough aircraft and airfields to begin a sustained offensive in November 1944.

Aircraft and infrastructure were two legs of the attacker's capabilities. Equally important were the weapons and tactics the attacker employed. These evolved throughout the campaign. The weapons included the different bombs, but also included electronic warfare, including airborne ground-tracking radar, electronic signal intelligence equipment, and radar-jamming electronics. Tactics involved bombing strategies and fighter escort tactics.

Aircraft

Probably in no other air campaign did the attacker use fewer types of aircraft than in the strategic bombing campaign against Japan. Only two types of aircraft were used over Japan: the B-29 bomber and the P-51 Mustang long-range fighter. Other aircraft types were used in support roles; in reconnaissance and rescue.

The Boeing B-29 Superfortress

The B-29 was the most capable bomber of World War II. Including prototypes, total production equaled 3,987 aircraft. The bomber remained in the Army Air Force and successor US Air Force inventory until 1960. The campaign against Japan was built around the B-29.

The aircraft was one of the biggest of World War II. Its wingspan was 141ft and fuselage 99ft long. It was fast: maximum speed was 357mph and it cruised at 290mph, speeds close to early-war fighter top speeds. It was powered by four Wright R-3350 Duplex-Cyclone engines. Twin-row radial engines, early versions generated 2,200hp.

The B-29 weighed 74,500lb empty. With a full load of fuel, bombs, and ammunition for ten .50-caliber machine guns and one 20mm cannon, its maximum take-off weight was 135,000lb. It could carry up to 22,000lb of bombs in its two bomb bays, although the normal load for a mission to Japan was closer to 10,000lb. It had an effective combat range of 3,200 miles. By trading fuel for bomb load it could increase that range by up to 1,000 miles. Its combat ceiling was 31,850ft.

Neither size nor carrying capacity alone made the B-29 the deadly weapon of war it was. It was the first combat aircraft designed to fight fully pressurized; allowing the crew to fly to targets in shirtsleeve conditions significantly reduced crew fatigue. It was the first bomber to be designed from the start to carry ground-mapping radar. One in four carried intercept receivers allowing them to detect enemy radar. A few carried communications search receivers. The B-29's turrets were remote-controlled, with primitive computers developing targeting solutions. Besides greatly increased accuracy the system allowed any gunner to target all four turrets.

The B-29 was imperfect. Its engines were temperamental, prone to overheating. The crankcase, made from a magnesium alloy, sometimes caught fire. A fully loaded B-29 was difficult to fly. Many crashed on takeoff, especially if an engine faltered. It was a complex aircraft, with many parts which could fail. More B-29s were lost due to mechanical issues than to enemy action. Yet once reliability was resolved the airplane became a war-winner.

The P-51 Mustang was one of the best fighters in the Army Air Force's inventory and the only one available in the spring of 1945 with the range to escort B-29s bombing Japan. (AC)

The North American P-51 Mustang

If the B-29 was the most capable bomber of World War II, the P-51 was the best all-around fighter of the war. It combined high speed, excellent reliability, long range, outstanding high-altitude performance, and superlative maneuverability. With six .50-caliber machine guns, it could destroy any Japanese fighter.

The Mustang was an almost accidental design. In 1940 RAF agents asked North American to build P-40s under license. The company offered its own single-engine fighter design equipped with an Allison engine, superior to the P-40. The British ordered 320, which were first delivered in January 1941.

Originally a fighter bomber, pairing the airframe with Rolls-Royce's Merlin engine gave the fighter high-altitude capability with low fuel consumption, transforming it into the war's best escort fighter. The Merlin engine Mustang had a ceiling of 41,900ft, a maximum speed of 440mph, and a cruising speed of 362mph. Its Packard engine, a licensed version of Britain's Merlin, produced 1,490hp, with a war emergency power rating of 1,720hp.

The Mustang entered the campaign late. Its range was 1,600 miles with external fuel tanks, around half the B-29's 3,200-mile range. Iwo Jima's capture finally provided a base within range of Japan for P-51s. By April 1945, Mustangs began escorting B-29s during daylight missions.

As with the B-29s, the P-51s were fighting at the very edge of their performance capabilities. The 750-mile trip to Japan was carried out by a one-man crew. During long overwater flights the fighters used a B-29 as a navigation aircraft. If the formation ran into storms it would scatter until through the clouds and then reform. If the storm was bad enough, fighters simply disappeared.

Other aircraft

By July 1945, the B-29s and P-51s of XXI Air Command were joined by Fifth Air Force fighters and bombers, including B-24s, B-25s, B-32s, and P-47s operating out of Okinawa. The southern parts of Kyushu were within range of these aircraft. They were mainly used to reduce Japan's military capabilities in advance of the expected invasion in November 1945, and played little role in strategic bombardment.

Four other aircraft participated indirectly in the strategic bombing campaign. The most important was the F-13, the photo reconnaissance version of the B-29. One hundred and eighteen were built. Each F-13 carried six cameras, extra ammunition, and gasoline. These aircraft conducted solo photo reconnaissance missions over Japan. While vulnerable to fighter interception, they were rarely attacked.

"Dumbos," long-range aircraft used for air-sea rescue, were also used. These were tasked with finding and rescuing B-29 and P-51 fliers whose aircraft ditched during the long flights to and from Japan. There were two types of Dumbo aircraft. Flying boats, such as the PBY Catalina and PBM Mariners, could land near ditched flyers and rescue them. Land-based bombers, including B-17 and B-29s, were also used on Dumbo missions. These aircraft carried an air-droppable lifeboat which could carry 15 people.

Basing and logistics

To start its strategic bombing campaign against Japan the Army Air Force needed to reach Japan. The B-29, with the longest range of any bomber in the United States Army Air Force's inventory, still lacked the range to reach Japan from any airfield held by the Allies in January 1944. The only territory held by the United States or its Allies close enough for B-29s to reach Japan was in central China.

But not just any airfield would suffice to handle B-29s. They needed a paved runway with a length of at least 8,000ft to take off safely. An 8,500ft runway was preferable. Such airfields existed in Europe and North America, and established Pacific bases like those at Hawaii. Before the campaign could start, airfields of such quality would have to be built to allow B-29 operations.

Since friendly territory existed in China, an airbase was built at Chengdu, deep in western China. It was built by hand, using peasant labor. From there, the B-29s could only reach Kyushu, the southernmost of the four Japanese Home Islands, and only with reduced bomb loads. Closer bases were needed.

The Marianas Islands were the solution. Located in the Central Pacific, these islands were close enough to easily reach most of Honshu and all of Kyushu and Shikoku, which constituted Japan's industrial belt. Japan held the Marianas as 1944 started: Saipan and Tinian had been a Japanese mandate since the end of World War I, and Guam, a US possession, was captured by Japan in 1941. The United States invaded and captured these islands in June and July 1944; Saipan first, followed by Guam and then Tinian. Once secured, airbases capable of hosting B-29s were built on all three. Five airfields for B-29s were built: one on Saipan, two on Guam, and two on Tinian.

The process was repeated on Iwo Jima after that island was captured in February 1945. Iwo Jima airfields were not intended to host B-29 combat missions against Japan, yet they could act as emergency landing fields for damaged B-29s and host the long-range P-51 Mustang fighters escorting B-29s. When the Ryuku Islands were captured in April 1945, additional emergency fields for B-29s and fighter strips for escorts were built, notably on Okinawa.

Building the airfields was not as simple as ordering them built. Limited construction personnel were available, and initially priority was given to harbor facilities, naval base installation, and facilities for ground troops. Even when priority reverted to building the very heavy bomber fields, problems remained. The construction troops had to contend with Japanese infiltrators. Armed guards were required to protect them.

Despite the chaos, the airfields came together. Isley Field on Saipan had an 8,500ft by 200ft runway by October 1944. A second was completed by December. A second planned

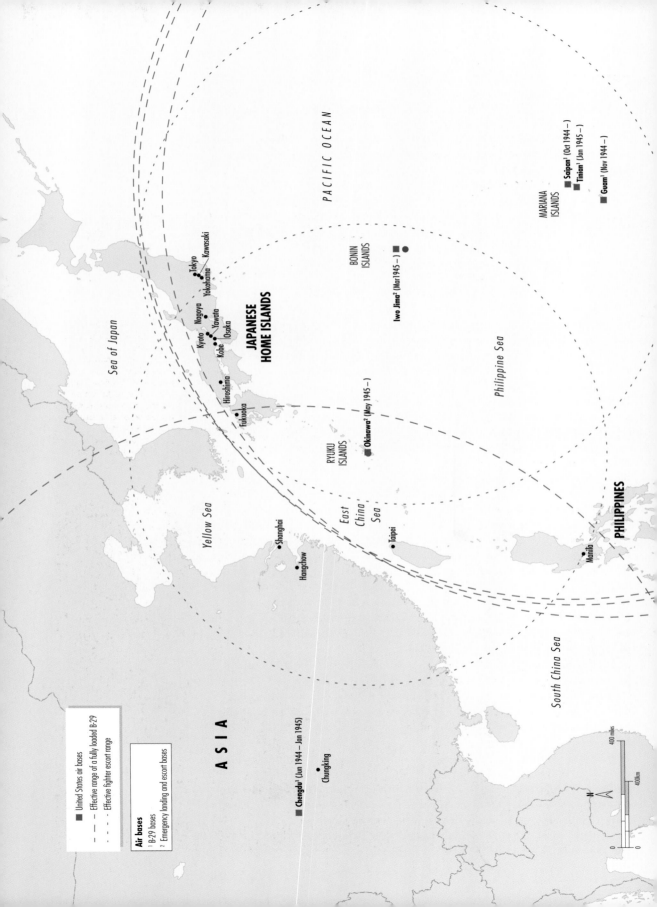

PACIFIC OCEAN

MARIANA
ISLANDS

■ **Saipan**[1] (Oct 1944 –)
■ **Tinian**[1] (Jan 1945 –)

■ **Guam**[1] (Nov 1944 –)

BONIN
ISLANDS

■ ●

Iwo Jima[2] (Mar 1945 –)

Tokyo
Kawasaki
Yokohama
Nagoya
Kyoto Yawata
Kobe Osaka

**JAPANESE
HOME ISLANDS**

Hiroshima

Fukuoka

Sea of Japan

Philippine Sea

● **Okinawa**[2] (May 1945 –)

RYUKU
ISLANDS

Yellow Sea

East
China
Sea

● Shanghai

● Hangchow

● Taipei

● Manila

PHILIPPINES

South China Sea

A S I A

■ **Chengdu**[1] (Jun 1944 – Jan 1945)

● Chungking

Air bases

■ United States air bases
– – – Effective range of a fully loaded B-29
· · · · Effective fighter escort range

[1] B-29 bases
[2] Emergency landing and escort bases

N

0   400 miles
0   400 km

OPPOSITE DAY 1: STRATEGIC OVERVIEW

B-29 airfield on Saipan was canceled, with extra runways added on Tinian as substitutes. The first two runways on Tinian were completed in January 1945. One additional runway was added each month from February through May for a total of six split between two airfields. Two airfields with two runways each were started on Guam in November 1944; the first was operational in February 1945, with the other three completed in May, June, and July.

Once the Marianas had been taken, the most formidable challenge to the campaign was logistics. A single B-29 fully loaded and fueled for a maximum-range mission to Japan required 34,000lb of 100-octane aviation gasoline. It carried a quarter-ton of machine gun and 20mm ammunition for its defensive guns and up to 8,000lb of bombs. Every ounce, as well as oil, grease, and spare parts for aircraft maintenance came from the United States.

The main reason bases in China were abandoned once the Marianas became available was logistics. Chengdu was almost on the other side of the globe from the United States, and all the supplies, except food and water had to be airlifted in. And due to the ranges and quantities involved, B-29s had to be used as transports. To mount one bombing mission against Japan a B-29 had to make nine round trips between India and Japan ferrying fuel and munitions for the combat mission.

The Marianas were closer than China, but the logistical challenges remained daunting. In addition to fuel and munitions, food for aircrew and ground staff had to be imported, as did virtually everything to build the airfields and maintenance facilities.

The March 9–10 1945 firebombing mission on Tokyo required over 6,600 tons of consumables, mostly fuel and bombs. The week of incendiary raids in March consumed nearly 9,500 tons of incendiaries, exhausting the supply until more could be brought from the United States.

Navy Construction Battalions (Seabees) and Army engineering units built B-29 airfields on three islands in the Marianas. Construction began before Japanese resistance ended. Army troops on Saipan are shown protecting engineers building an airfield on Guam from Japanese snipers. (USAAF)

Those missions involved only 330 aircraft. By June 500-aircraft missions were being flown and by August a single day could see over 800 B-29s take off from the Marianas. This would have consumed most of the 16,300 deadweight tons of fuel carried by one T2 tanker.

Logistics explain why strategic bombing was largely restricted to B-29s, even after bases in Okinawa and Iwo Jima brought the B-17 and B-24 within range of Japan. A single B-29 could carry two to four times the bomb load of the smaller bombers with the same-sized crew as a B-17 or B-24. It also explains why B-29s remained based in the Marianas after the occupation of Iwo Jima: the logistical price of building airfields capable of maintaining combat operations with B-29s was too high. It was more effectively used as a fighter field and emergency landing facility for the bombers.

Weapons and tactics

The B-29 was a bomb delivery platform intended to conduct high-altitude precision bombing. Flying at altitudes which placed it above flak, which enemy fighters found difficult to reach and at which they performed poorly, the Superfortress was supposed to be able to accurately hit targets of military significance, particularly factories and armories.

On these missions it carried high-explosive general-purpose bombs. The standard general-purpose (GP) bombs used by the Army Air Force were the AN-M57 250lb bomb, AN-M64 500lb bomb, AN-M65 1,000lb bomb, and AN-M66 2,000lb bomb. In all just over half the weight of the bomb was casing, with explosive making up the balance. Initially, 500lb bombs were generally carried for strategic bombardment of factories or industrial facilities. These bombs were heavy enough to destroy buildings or industrial machinery, but light enough for many to be carried. Since even with the most accurate aiming bombs scattered, the more bombs that were dropped the more likely some would hit the target. Later larger bombs, including the 4,000lb AN-M56 blockbuster, were used to destroy reinforced concrete buildings in the most modern factories.

South Airfield (formerly Japanese Airfield # 1) on Iwo Jima. Mount Suribachi is in the background. The Iwo Jima airfields provided a base for escorting P-51 Mustangs and a place for battle-damaged B-29s to land. Note the wrecked Superfortresses in the foreground. (USNHHC)

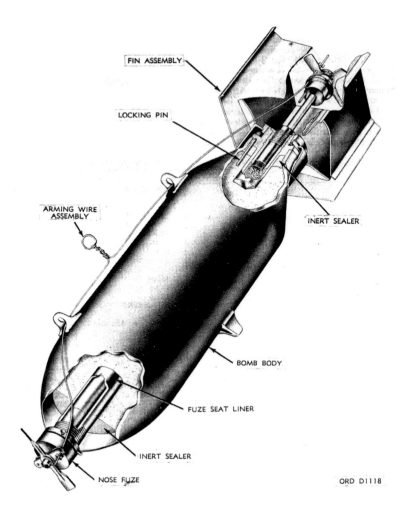

FIN ASSEMBLY

LOCKING PIN

ARMING WIRE
ASSEMBLY

INERT SEALER

BOMB BODY

FUZE SEAT LINER

INERT SEALER

NOSE FUZE

ORD D1118

Cutaway drawing of a
standard general-purpose
(GP) high-explosive bomb.
These came in 500lb,
1,000lb, 2,000lb, and
4,000lb sizes. (AC)

Using B-29s for daylight formation bombing from 30,000ft usually yielded poor results. A major complication was the jet stream, discovered in the 1930s and still poorly understood in 1945. Narrow high-altitude currents of air, jet streams moved at speeds between 60 and 250mph. The most powerful jet stream, the polar jet, frequently crossed Japan at altitudes between 30,000 and 39,000ft.

When targets were under a jet stream, which could be 100–200 miles wide, accurate bombing was almost impossible. Bombs would be scattered by wind sheer. Even if the jet stream was absent, accurate visual bombing was difficult. Low-level clouds or smoke frequently obscured targets, forcing reliance on radar-directed bombing. Early in the campaign, when less sophisticated ground-track radar was used and radar operators lacked experience, bombing accuracy using radar was poor. If the target was near a water landmark it could be recognized; otherwise it was invisible.

Due to the poor results by high-altitude daylight bombing, Curtis LeMay switched to low- and medium-level area bombing using incendiaries. These missions were flown at night, at altitudes between 6,000 and 14,000ft, primarily using M-47, M-69, and M-74 incendiary bombs, with a few other incendiary types thrown in.

The M-47, made from thin sheet metal, was originally a chemical weapon, to be filled with poison gas or white phosphorous. Against Japan it was filled with napalm or napalm and

Crosswind

Upwind

Downwind

OPPOSITE JET STREAM EFFECTS ON HIGH-ALTITUDE BOMBING

At 30,000ft, the intended operating altitude for the B-29 Superfortress, bombers frequently found themselves caught in the jet stream when attacking targets in Japan. Jet stream winds ranged from 100 to 200mph, disrupting bombing accuracy regardless of the approach taken. Even if jet stream winds did not scatter the bombs as they were dropped, they caused the following problems (these examples assume a jet stream speed of 150mph).

Downwind Approach:
If the bomb run was made with the jet stream the combined speed of the bomber (290mph) and the jet stream (150mph) would yield a ground speed of 440mph. Advantage: Antiaircraft artillery found it difficult to target bombers moving at that speed. Disadvantage: The bombsight could not compensate for the ground speed, and bombs would miss.

Upwind Approach:
If the bomb run was made into the jet stream the combined speed of the bomber (290mph) into the jet stream (150mph) headwind would yield a ground speed of 140mph. Advantage: The bombsight could accurately aim traveling at that ground speed. Disadvantage: Japanese antiaircraft artillery could also accurately target the bombers, even at 30,000ft. Unacceptable casualties would result.

Crosswind approach:
If the bomb run was made perpendicular to the jet stream the bombers had to start the bomb run 30 degrees upwind of the target, as the jet stream would blow them off course. The crosswind yielded a ground speed near 325mph, but also meant the bombs would be blown sideways. Advantage: The aircraft were moving fast enough to make it difficult for antiaircraft artillery. Disadvantage: The bombsight could not compensate for the crosswind deflection. The bombs would miss.

phosphorus. The filled weight of one of these bombs was 115lb. The M-69 and M-74 were steel pipes, 8in long and 3in in diameter with a hexagonal cross section. Each weighed around 6lb. These were packaged in clusters of 40–60 incendiaries. The containers would open at 2,000ft, scattering the bomblets, which ignited on impact. The M-69 had a cotton streamer to stabilize the bomb. Its successor, the M-74, omitted the streamer, replacing the weight with more napalm.

Typically, M-47s were dropped at the beginning of a fire raid, to start "appliance fires," – fires severe enough to require dispatch of a fire engine. The smaller M-69 bombs were dropped once fire departments' resources were fully committed, creating a large number of small fires. Often a few 500lb general-purpose bombs were added to discourage fire-fighting.

LeMay's use of area bombing was virtually viewed as heresy by some Army Air Force precision bombing advocates. But the tactic was stunningly effective. LeMay did not abandon daylight precision bombing. Rather, he mixed precision bombing and area bombing. When weather forecasts predicted clear weather suitable for precision bombing, daylight precision raids were scheduled. When cloudy weather was forecast, nighttime area bombing was carried out. As the ineffectiveness of Japanese airborne interception and antiaircraft artillery became apparent, daylight missions were conducted at lower altitudes, typically 20,000 to 25,000ft, increasing accuracy.

LeMay also committed doctrinal heresy by enthusiastically supporting using B-29s for aerial mining of Japanese harbors and seaways. Three types of mines were dropped: the Mark 25, Mark 26, and Mark 36 naval mine. All three mines were US Navy ordnance. The Mark 25 weighed 2,000lb; both the Mark 26 and Mark 36 weighed 1,000lb. The mines were armed with different fuses, including a number of low-frequency acoustic mines, viewed as unsweepable. B-29s carried up to 12 1,000lb mines, seven 2,000lb mines, or a mix of both not to exceed 14,000lb.

The final and most famous type of bomb carried by B-29s was the atomic bomb. Two were dropped: a uranium bomb (Little Boy) on Hiroshima and a plutonium bomb (Fat Man) on Nagasaki. That was the total inventory of atomic bombs available in August 1945. More were being manufactured, but the next one would not have been available until November.

The US used several innovative tactics during the campaign. One involved the fighter escort once available. LeMay had fighters fly ahead of the daylight bomber formations, preventing Japanese fighters from attacking the bombers head-on. When they tried, they

Designed as a chemical warfare bomb, the M-47 was converted to an incendiary bomb by filling it with napalm instead of poison gas. The purple ring indicates it is an incendiary. The "A" version had thicker walls to prevent leaking. (PSAM)

ended up engaging US fighters instead. Japanese interceptors were forced to attack the bombers from behind, where their slow closing rate made them easy targets for the computer-compensated guns of the bomber formation.

The B-29 also used electronic countermeasures (ECM) to stymie Japanese searchlight- and fire-control radar. This included jamming radars aboard bombers and "rope," 400ft rolls of metal foil. These tools were first used in an April 1945 mission. They proved so effective that each bomb wing modified four bombers as electronic countermeasures aircraft, carrying multiple jammers instead of bombs. These "guardian angels" reduced losses dramatically.

DEFENDER'S CAPABILITIES
Home defense

Japan's defenders had an easier task than the United States bombers attempting to knock Japan out of the war. The Japanese were on their home turf, literally in the skies where their pilots trained. The United States had little knowledge of Japan, including the location and appearance of key industrial facilities. Japan had adequate airfields. The US bombers were attacking at the limits of their range, initially out of range of fighter escort. Japanese pilots could bail out of a damaged aircraft, land on their home soil and be in the cockpit of a new fighter within the day. American aircrew faced capture or an open ocean landing. Merely damaging B-29s often left them unable to complete the long overwater return trip to safety. The Japanese radar network warned defenders when the US bombers were coming, and what the probable target was. The US bombers did not know where Japanese interceptors were until the B-29s were attacked.

Despite all its advantages Japan was decisively defeated by the United States, suffering the worst aerial drubbing any industrialized world power had experienced. Its defeat was caused by more than enemy superiority or attacker competence. Rather, the Japanese too often failed to capitalize on their capabilities and strengths, not using the aircraft available, the facilities, and infrastructure they possessed to best effect, and most especially using the wrong weapons and tactics against their foes.

Aircraft

Japan had enough fighters to defend Japan, but never assigned enough to home defense. Between the start of the US strategic bombing in June 1944 and the war's end Japan averaged 2,350 total operational fighters monthly, yet rarely was more than one-sixth assigned to home defense. During the critical period between October 1944 and March 1945, only 375–385 fighters were assigned to home defense. After April home defense fighter numbers increased, with the number reaching 535 by August. By then, Japan's home defense was

A Kawanishi N1K *Shiden*. Code-named George by the Allies, it was the most dangerous fighter threat faced by the B-29s. This picture was taken in Japan shortly after the Japanese surrender. (NMUSAF)

A Nakajima Ki-44 *Shoki* photographed on a captured Japanese airfield in the Philippines. Code-named Tojo, the *Shoki* was the first Japanese single-engine fighter with at least four heavy-caliber machine guns. It was intended as a bomber interceptor. (AC)

facing B-29s, their escorting fighters, and other Allied aircraft which could reach southern Kyushu from Okinawa bases. These Japanese fighters could be divided into three broad categories: late-war single-engine fighters, early war single-engine fighters, and night fighters.

Late-war single-engine fighters

These included the Kawasaki Ki-61 *Hien* ("flying swallow" – Allied code-name Tony), Nakajima Ki-84 *Hayate* ("gale" – Allied code-name Frank), Mitsubishi J2M *Raiden* ("thunderbolt" – Allied code-name Jack), and Kawanishi N1K-J *Shiden* ("violet lightning" – Allied code-name George). *Hien* and *Hayate* were Army aircraft; *Raiden* and *Shiden* Navy aircraft.

All four first flew in 1943, and were introduced operationally in 1944. *Hein* had the two 7.9mm machine gun and two 20mm cannon armament of the early-war fighters, but the others had four cannon or two cannon and two 12.7mm machine guns, a little light for downing four-engine bombers, but equal to the firepower of late-war Allied fighters.

The aircraft were also armored, and except for the *Hein* had powerplants comparable to those of the latest generation Allied fighters. All had good high-altitude performance. The *Hein* and *Raiden* were relatively slow, with top speeds of 360mph and 370mph respectively, but the *Hayate* and *Shiden* could top 400mph.

These aircraft all suffered from poor reliability, but the main problem with all four was there were not enough. *Hayate* production topped 3,400 aircraft; around 3,000 *Hein* were built, 1,500 *Shiden*, and less than 700 *Raiden*. Production plunged in 1945 as bombing disrupted both the factories and distribution networks feeding parts to factories.

Early-war single-engine fighters

Japan started the war with some of the finest fighter aircraft available: the Mitsubishi A6M Zero (Allied code-name Zeke), Nakajima Ki-43 *Hayabusa* ("peregrine falcon" – Allied code-name Oscar), and the Nakajima Ki-44 *Shoki* ("Zhong Kui," a mythological demon vanquisher – Allied code-name Tojo). The Zero and *Hayabusa* outclassed any 1941 and 1942 Allied fighter in the Pacific theater. The Zero was a Navy fighter, the premier carrier fighter of the Japanese Navy, while the *Hayabusa* and *Shoki* were Army aircraft.

Yet the Zero and *Hayabusa* had significant weaknesses. Neither had armor or self-sealing gasoline tanks. Lightly built, they disintegrated when damaged. While outstanding aircraft at low and medium altitudes, they performed poorly at high altitudes. They were slow by 1945 standards. The top speed of the Zero was 346mph; the *Hayabusa* could not exceed 333mph in level flight. Both were also poorly armed. The Zero had two 7.7mm machine guns and two low-velocity 20mm cannon; the *Hayabusa* mounted two 12.7mm machine guns. This was unlikely to shoot down, or even severely damage a B-29 in one pass, and the bombers generally moved too fast to permit a second pass.

The *Shoki* was a little better equipped to fight Superfortresses. Designed as a bomber interceptor, it was armed with either four 12.7mm machine guns or two 12.7mm machine guns and two 20mm cannon. A few mounted two 40mm cannon instead of the 20mm cannon. Yet it shared some weaknesses of other early fighters. It was relatively lightly built with a maximum speed of 376mph. While it had a good rate of climb, it had been intended to intercept high-level bomber formations when a high formation was 24,000 to 28,000ft. It had a service ceiling of 36,000ft, but was sluggish above 30,000ft, the height at which many B-29s operated.

The Zero and *Hayabusa* were the most produced Japanese aircraft. Over 11,000 Zeroes were built and nearly 6,000 *Hayabusa*s. Production continued until the end of the war. Ill-suited for use against high-flying and fast Superfortresses, they were often used because nothing else was available. The *Shoki* was built in smaller batches: only 1,200 were built, production ending in January 1945 in favor of the superior *Hayate*.

Twin-engine night fighters

Japan had three main night fighters: the Kawasaki Ki-45 *Toryu* ("dragon slayer" – Allied code-name Nick), Kawasaki Ki-102 (Allied code-name Randy), and Nakajima J1N1 *Gekko* ("moonlight" – Allied code-name Irving). Japan also produced a night-fighter version of the Yokosuka P1Y *Ginga* ("galaxy" – Allied code-name Frances) bomber, but only 97 were produced, and due to poor high-altitude performance most were converted back to bombers. The *Toryu* and Ki-102 were built for the Army; *Gekko* and *Ginga* were Navy aircraft.

Toryu and *Gekko* were contemporaries with similar performance. Both were designed in the late 1930s, entering service in late 1941 and early 1942. They had a top speed of 336mph and 315mph respectively, and were barely able to fly high enough to catch B-29s at 30,000ft. Both were heavily armed. *Toryu* carried one forward-firing 37mm and 20mm cannon; *Gekko* carried a mix of up to four upward- or downward-firing 20mm cannon.

Both had originally been developed as long-range escorts, but were converted to night fighters once airborne radar sets became available. They were large enough to take the sets, and too slow to be effective daytime fighters. Poor training for the radar operators and poor radar performance handicapped them. They were also handicapped by small numbers: only 1,700 *Toryu* and fewer than 500 *Gekko* were built, many early in the war.

The Ki-102 was a replacement for the *Toryu*, entering service in 1944. It had a top speed of 360mph and a 32,000ft ceiling. Superior to earlier night fighters, only 200 entered service before the war ended.

Air defense system

Japan possessed the potential to stop the United States strategic bombing offensive even with the limited numbers of fighters it had available. It had the resources to employ its fighters effectively, and significant numbers of other assets with which to repel an air assault: an

The Nakajima J1N1 *Gekko* was the Imperial Japanese Navy's night fighter. Designed in the late 1930s, its top speed of 315mph meant it could barely keep up with the Superfortress at the B-29's cruising speed of 290mph. (AC)

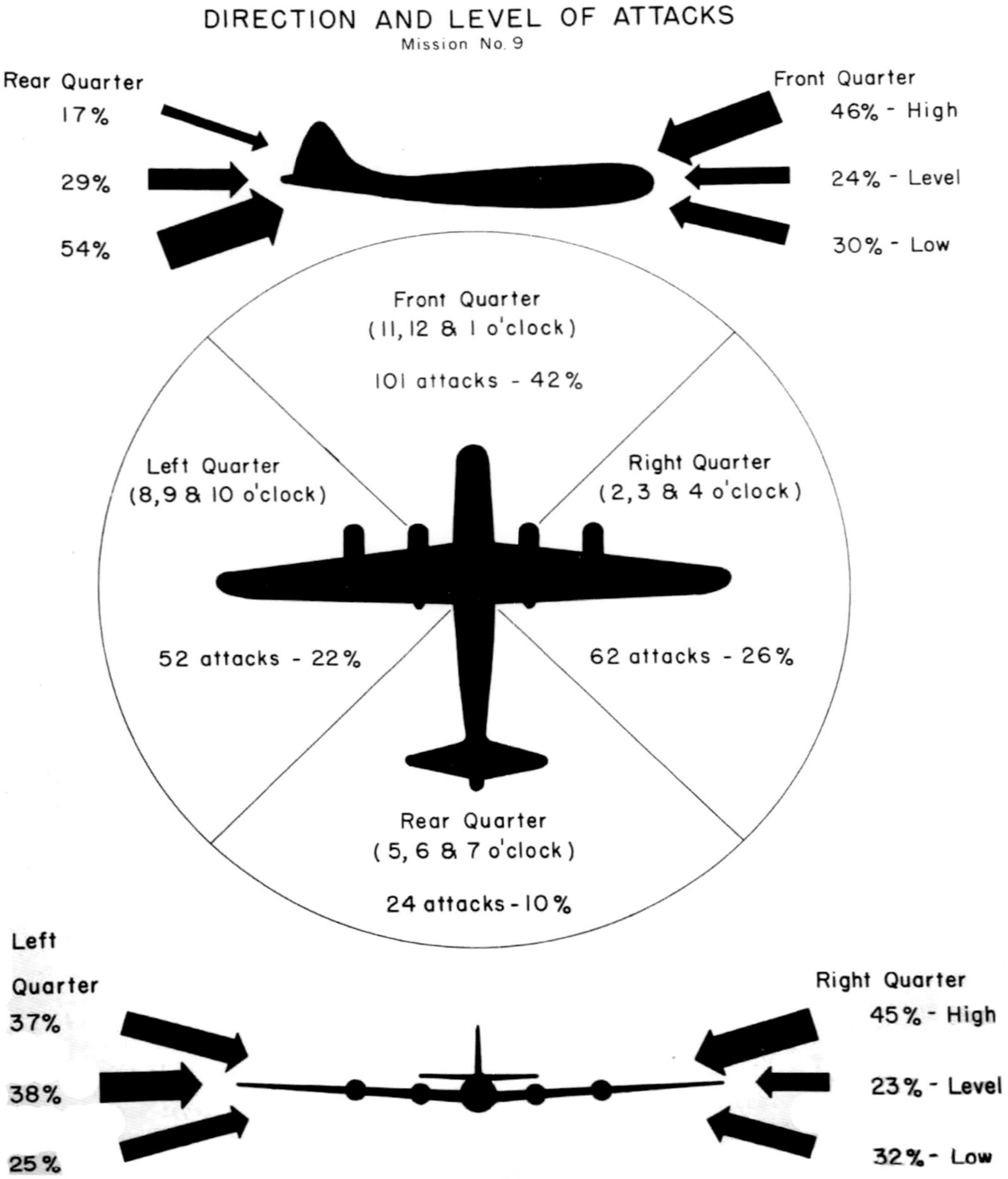

DIRECTION AND LEVEL OF ATTACKS
Mission No. 9

Rear Quarter
17%

29%

54%

Front Quarter
46% - High

24% - Level

30% - Low

Front Quarter
(11, 12 & 1 o'clock)

101 attacks - 42%

Left Quarter
(8, 9 & 10 o'clock)

52 attacks - 22%

Right Quarter
(2, 3 & 4 o'clock)

62 attacks - 26%

Rear Quarter
(5, 6 & 7 o'clock)

24 attacks - 10%

Left
Quarter
37%

38%

25%

Right Quarter
45% - High

23% - Level

32% - Low

Japanese fighters preferred to attack B-29s from ahead and above. This diagram, from a B-29 combat crew manual, presents Japanese fighter attacks during an unescorted daytime mission over China. Two-fifths of the attacks were head-on passes; nearly half from above. (AC)

adequate early warning radar network and large numbers of antiaircraft guns and searchlights, many of which were radar directed.

Japan did not have to defend the entire Home Islands. In the 1940s Japan's population and industry clustered in a belt 100–150 miles wide running roughly from Tokyo to Nagasaki. This included the southeast coast of Honshu, a strip of northern Shikoku, and northwestern Kyushu. Hokkaido, northern Honshu, and southern Kyushu were largely sources for raw materials.

Japan's military airfield network was concentrated in this region, to provide proximity to the population and industrial output needed to man these bases and be near aircraft factories. Japan failed to produce adequate numbers of antiaircraft artillery. Including prewar stocks and wartime construction, fewer than 7,000 heavy antiaircraft artillery – 75mm to 127mm – were produced. But they still possessed enough to protect their cities. Tokyo was ringed by nearly 400 heavy antiaircraft guns.

By 1944 Japan had developed and deployed an array of ground-based radar. This included early-warning radar, and searchlight- and antiaircraft gun-control radar. While Japan lacked an early warning system completely ringing the country, the system provided continuous coverage from the north coast of Hokkaido, the entire Pacific coast of the Home Islands, and the Sea of Japan coast of Kyushu. Only the western coast of Japan was not covered by radar. No Allied airbases existed from which even B-29s could approach from that direction.

Yet these resources were not used effectively.

The first problem was duplication of effort: there was an Imperial Army and an Imperial Navy version of everything. Some specialization was justified. Carrier aircraft have different needs to land-based aircraft. Shipboard surface search and fire-control radar operates under different conditions and environments than land-based fire control radar. Yet both the Army and Navy independently developed land-based early-warning radar. Neither service cooperated with the other, delaying deployment of operational systems. Mistakes were duplicated; each service independently discovered the same problems.

Once operational, each service deployed an independent early-warning network, often with Army and Navy stations located a few miles apart. An integrated joint-service early-warning network would have allowed Japan to be ringed by radar coverage.

Similar rivalry and duplication existed in every aspect of air defense. Both services operated independent fighter and air defense systems. The Imperial Army assumed primary responsibility for the air defense of the Home Islands, while the Navy deployed its air defense almost exclusively to defend naval bases, fleet anchorages, and shipyards.

Worse, active air defense was organized geographically. Army fighters were in air divisions which belonged to field armies, and generally stayed within the army's geographic boundaries. Navy aircraft remained tied to the immediate area where its fleet was assigned. As a result, while having 300–400 fighters stationed throughout southern Japan, no more than 70 could meet an attack.

A B-29 raid against Tokyo would be attacked by fighters in the 10th Flying Division in central Honshu. Fighters assigned to the 23rd Flying Brigade in the adjacent army covering Nagoya typically could not fly to Tokyo and join the fight. Naval aircraft at Kure would not respond to a US raid against Kobe, only about 150 miles away. The other city was outside their area of responsibility.

Japanese radar also proved easy to jam. The fragmented radar development program led the Japanese to use a narrow band of frequencies for both gun-laying and searchlight-control radars. US jamming aircraft quickly found those frequencies, leaving the air defenses blind.

Japan never trained adequate numbers of pilots. Prewar training focused on developing a small number of highly trained pilots, with high washout rates. Training output was not significantly expanded during the war's early days. When training programs finally expanded, Japan was short of aviation gasoline, lacking fuel to adequately train pilots.

The majority of Japan's heavy antiaircraft artillery were 75mm guns, like the one pictured in this drawing. It had a maximum altitude of 30,000ft. (AC)

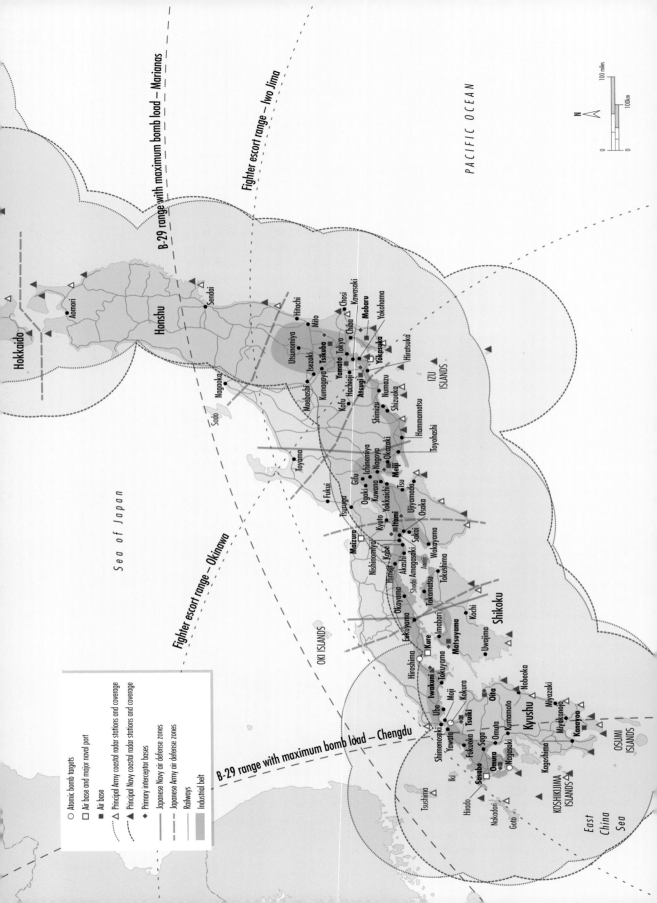

B-29 range with maximum bomb load – Marianas

Fighter escort range – Iwo Jima

PACIFIC OCEAN

N

100 miles

100km

Hokkaido

Aomori

Honshu

Sendai

Sea of Japan

Hitachi

Mito

Utsunomiya
Maebashi
Isezaki
Kumagaya
Tsukuba
Kofu
Hachioji
Yamato
Tokyo
Chosi
Chiba
Kawasaki
Mobaru
Yokohama
Atsugi
Yokosuka
Hiratsuka
Numazu
Shizuoka
Shimizu
Hammamatsu
Toyohashi

Nagaoka

Soto

Toyama

Fukui

IZU
ISLANDS

Tsuruga

Gifu
Ogaki
Ichinomiya
Nagoyo
Kuwana
Kyoto
Yokkaichi
Okazaki
Meiji
Tsu
Ujiyamada
Izumi
Osaka
Sakai
Wakayama

Maizuru
Nishinomiya
Himeji
Kobe
Akashi
Shodo
Amagasaki
Awaji
Takamatsu
Tokushima

Fighter escort range – Okinawa

OKI ISLANDS

Okayama

Fukuyama
Imabari
Matsuyama
Kochi
Uwajima

Shikoku

Hiroshima
Kure
Iwakuni
Tokuyama
Kokura
Moji
Ube
Kura
Tsuiki
Oita
Nobeoka

Shimonoseki
Yawata
Fukuoka
Saga
Omuta
Kumamoto
Miyazaki
Miyakonojo
Kanoya

Iki

Nagasaki
Omura
Sasabo

Kyushu

Kagoshima

Tsushima

Hirado

Nakadori
Goto

KOSHIKIJIMA
ISLANDS

OSUMI
ISLANDS

East
China
Sea

B-29 range with maximum bomb load – Chengdu

Legend:
- ○ Atomic bomb targets
- □ Air base and major naval port
- ■ Air base
- △ Principal Army coastal radar stations and coverage
- ▲ Principal Navy coastal radar stations and coverage
- ◆ Primary interceptor bases
- Japanese Navy air defense zones
- Japanese Army air defense zones
- Railways
- Industrial belt

Finally, Japan never developed an integrated air defense plan or interception system. It had a multi-layered system for detecting incoming US attacks. Signal intelligence provided advance warning of raids, monitoring pre-mission radio checks to learn when raids were imminent. A chain of picket boats provided (at least for the Navy) advance warning of missions, and an early-warning radar chain to warn when the bombers were an hour out. But it then failed to adequately use the information.

Early-warning radar never provided information on attack altitudes. When LeMay varied approach altitudes, interceptors were caught thousands of feet above or below the bomber formation. No integrated operations rooms (like those used by the RAF and Luftwaffe) existed. Ground control did not vector fighters to intercept the bombers. Instead, word was passed to groups or air regiments, which launched aircraft independently. Instead of coordinated attacks by large groups of fighters, US formations faced multiple attacks by between ten and 40 interceptors.

Air-to-ground communications was poor. Night fighters were frequently sent in the anticipated direction of incoming bombers and then expected to use onboard radar to find targets. Japanese aircraft lacked Identification-Friend-or-Foe (IFF) beacons, so did not know whether a radar contact was a target. And there was no coordination between Army and Navy.

Weapons and tactics

Japanese aircraft were armed with a variety of machine guns and cannon. The 7.9mm machine gun, equivalent to American .30-caliber or British .303 machine guns, was used on early war fighters and the *Hein*. A rifle-caliber gun, it dated to World War I. It was mounted as in their World War I predecessors: in the nose of the aircraft, synchronized to fire through the propeller arc. In late-war fighters it was replaced by heavier 12.7mm (.50-caliber) machine guns.

The Japanese used a variety of aerial cannon. Early-war Zeroes had two wing-mounted low-velocity Type 99 Mark 1 20mm cannon, with a low muzzle velocity and only a 60-round magazine. Later model Zeroes and late-war Navy fighters used the Type 99 Mark 2 20mm. It had a higher muzzle velocity and a 100-round magazine. The Army equipped its aircraft with Ho-1, Ho-3, and Ho-5 20mm cannon. The first two were developed from an antitank gun, while the Ho-5 was developed from foreign autocannon and was equivalent to 20mm aerial cannon used by the Allies.

Japan developed a 40mm aerial cannon intended for use against bombers. Using caseless ammunition, (which reduced weight and permitted a good rate of fire) its range was only 150 meters, limiting its effectiveness.

The 7.9mm machine gun was a fine weapon against wood and fabric aircraft of the 1930s, but relatively ineffective against late-war armored metal fighters and bombers, as was the Type 99 Mark 1 cannon. The other weapons were comparable to Allied late-war armament, but too few were carried. Allied fighters carried six or eight .50-caliber machine guns or four cannon; Japanese fighters carried four machine guns or two machine guns and two cannon, which was inadequate against B-29s.

Operational limitations dictated fighter tactics against B-29 formations. The preferred attack on a B-29 was from ahead and above. This brought fighters against the heaviest defensive firepower (B-29 forward, upper turrets had four .50-caliber machine guns, compared to the two that the other turrets had), but a closing rate in excess of 600mph in head-on attacks provided only a short time for the bombers' gunners to react, and complicated deflection fire from B-29s in the formation other than the one targeted. Head-on attacks also allowed an extremely close zero-deflection shot at a B-29 – the only attack likely to bring down the big bombers.

A table showing fire envelopes of Japanese antiaircraft artillery developed by US intelligence. Antiaircraft guns only reach maximum altitude when firing directly overhead. Effective range is 90 percent of its maximum range, roughly the altitude reached at 60 degrees elevation. (AC)

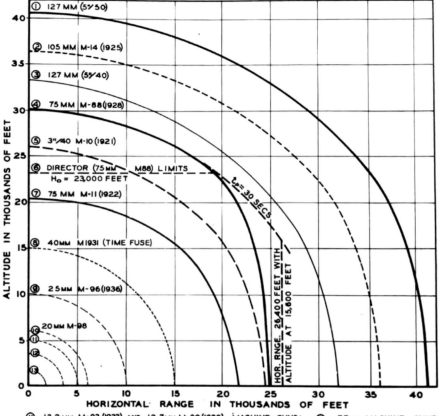

It was difficult to position fighters for a head-on attack. When the B-29s were at extreme altitude, most Japanese fighters were at their performance limit. Fighters had to climb above the B-29, positioning themselves ahead of the formation. The B-29's speed made this difficult even against unescorted bombers. Head-on attacks became almost impossible once Mustangs began escorting the bombers in April 1945.

The Japanese were so desperate to stop the B-29s that they organized a "special attack unit" of *Heins*. These aircraft were to ram B-29s but were not intended as suicide attacks: the pilots were expected to bail out after the collision. This tactic was successful against unescorted bombers. Some pilots actually knocked down multiple Superfortresses by ramming. Since these *Heins* were stripped of armor and weapons to improve performance, they became ineffective once bombers had fighter escorts.

Japan also had performance issues with its antiaircraft artillery. Only the Type 3 120mm gun and the 100mm M-14 was effective against B-29s at extreme altitudes. The combined total of both types was under 200 barrels. The Type 99 88mm antiaircraft gun could reach 34,000ft. Japan had 1,000 of them, with most retained for home defense. The rest of Japan's

heavy antiaircraft guns were various models of 75mm or 76mm guns, with ceilings between 20,000 and 30,000ft.

Antiaircraft artillery was viewed as a defensive weapon, and priority was given to manufacturing shells for offensive artillery. Enough antiaircraft shells existed to engage aircraft spotted visually, by searchlights, or by radar. However, there was too little ammunition for blind barrage firing, which proved effective against bomber formations in Europe. When the searchlight-control and gunnery-controlled radar was jammed – as occurred with increasing frequency after April 1945 – the antiaircraft guns fell silent.

Japan's firefighters were also a defensive weapon protecting Japan's cities, which were vulnerable to fire. Yet fire departments were small, firefighting equipment deficient, firefighters ill-trained, and water supplies inadequate. Fire departments were sufficient to control routine firefighting in peacetime (largely due to strict fire prevention efforts, including placing liability on property owners if fires damaged that of neighbors). There were insufficient fire engines and firefighters to cope with an incendiary attack. Tokyo, a city with a population in excess of six million, had only four ladder trucks for the whole city.

Assured by Japan's military that the Japanese homeland would never be attacked, municipal authorities procrastinated over civil defense preparation. Only after the Marianas fell were civilian-defense organizations created, air raid shelters constructed, or passive fire defenses (such as firebreaks and fire lanes) prepared. Frequently these proved inadequate. Shelters were too shallow, and did not protect against asphyxiation when fires consumed all breathable oxygen. Firebreaks failed to stop fire spreading when incendiaries were dropped on both sides of the break.

CAMPAIGN OBJECTIVES
Endgame in the Pacific

The Allied ability to quickly construct airfields on isolated Pacific islands permitted the United States to attack Japan from the air. Virtually the entire island of Tinian was turned into airfields, with West Field at one end and North Field (pictured here) at the other. (USNHHC)

As 1944 began ultimate Allied victory was not a certainty, but it was obvious the Axis were on the defensive. Italy had left the Axis and joined the Allies. The Western Allies occupied Corsica, Sardinia, Sicily, and the southern part of the Italian boot. They were preparing their spring 1944 invasion of France. The Soviet Union was driving west in offensives that relieved the siege of Leningrad and recaptured most of Ukraine.

Against Japan progress was less apparent, due to the greater geographical and logistical challenges offered by that theater. Yet progress was present. The British, under General William Slim, were taking the offensive in Burma, the aerial siege of Rabaul in New Britain was entering its final, successful stage, and General Douglas McArthur was retaking New Guinea's Huon Peninsula. In the Central Pacific, Admiral Chester Nimitz and US naval and land forces were completing their occupation of the Marshall Islands. In January 1944, Japan was on the offensive only in China.

Both sides realized the Allies could not emerge victorious without occupying the Axis homelands. Germany's eventual doom seemed sealed. Even without an invasion of France, the Soviet Red Army was moving west and would eventually reach Germany. Japan's fate seemed less certain. As 1944 opened, it was still out of reach, even with the soon-to-be operational B-29 Superfortress.

As long as Japan's industrial capabilities remained intact both sides realized any attempt to subdue Japan would be futile, especially if Japan retained uninterrupted access to resources from Manchukuo (as Japan named China's Manchuria). Should the Allies capture islands close enough to stage an invasion of the Japanese Home Islands, the Allies would still have to fight a massive amphibious campaign at the end of a long logistical chain. Japan would be fighting from its home soil, with short supply lines. Before invading, the Allies had to destroy Japan's industry. This required strategic bombardment.

In January 1944, Japan's war planners still counted on geography to shelter Japan. Before the United States could mount a strategic bombardment campaign it needed to build bomber bases in China, or occupy Japanese-held territory – the Marianas Islands, the Kurile Islands, or the Philippines. Japan felt it could repel any invasion of these. If the United States built bases in China, Japan believed it could advance and capture Chinese territory to neutralize the bomber bases. Even if the United States *did* capture an island base, say in the Marianas, the distances the bombers then had to travel remained formidable obstacles.

By January 1944, US military chiefs had plans in train to do what Japan considered impossible – build bases close enough to Japan to send strategic bombers against Japanese industry. The objective of the campaign was simple: to support an invasion of the Japanese Home Islands by destroying Japan's industrial base through strategic bombardment. Those actually conducting the bombing were more ambitious. They wanted to force Japan's surrender through strategic bombardment – not just to render a ground invasion unnecessary, but to demonstrate the potential of air power.

Allied plans for ending the war
Planning for a strategic bombing campaign against Japan started in 1943. It became apparent the B-29 would be unavailable to participate in the pre-invasion bombardment of Europe. The Superfortress seemed better suited to help defeat Japan than against Germany. Its long range and large bomb load offered the opportunity to start strategic bombing of Japan's Home Islands six months to a year earlier than would be possible with either the B-17s or B-24s.

There was no single objective or plan for the strategic bombardment of Japan. Rather, a series of objectives and plans evolved as capabilities evolved, geopolitical and military realities changed, and opportunities emerged. Organizations were developed rapidly and plans altered to exploit opportunities to test concepts and strategy and strike Japan's industry early.

By the Quadrant Conference, held at Quebec in August 1943, General "Hap" Arnold, commanding the Army Air Forces, presented a proposal to begin strategic bombing of Japan from bases in eastern China, supplied from India.

Arnold's Quadrant proposal was developed from a draft plan to use B-29s to attack Japan. The aircraft would be strategic assets run out of Washington DC. The original plans

The Allies lacked a land route to China in spring 1944. Except for water and local food, every pound of supplies had to be flown over the Himalaya Mountains, the tallest in the world. Fuel for the return trip also had to be flown in, further limiting supplies. (USAAF)

Major General Haywood S. "Possum" Hansell Jr. first commanded XXI Bomber Command. A precision bombardment purist, he resisted attempts to use B-29s for aerial mining or area bombing missions. A lack of visible results led to Hansell's replacement by Curtis LeMay. (AC)

envisioned four B-29 bomber commands, the XX through XXIII, independent of theater commanders. XX Bomber Command would operate out of China, the XXI would be stationed in the Marianas, the XXII would be assigned to Luzon in the Philippines, and the XXIII Shemya Island in the Aleutians and later, perhaps, the Kurile Islands. All four commands would be part of the Twentieth Air Force.

The plan allowed Japan to be attacked from multiple directions. Each command would contain three or four B-29 wings. Only China was controlled by Allied forces when this plan was developed. The Marianas were still protected by the Japanese-held Marshall Islands, Luzon was at the end of a long road of Japanese-held territory, Kiska was still in Japanese hands, and the Aleutians were too far from Japan to be reached by B-29s.

That led to Arnold's revision, presented at Quadrant. At the Cairo Conference, held in November 1943, planners decided to use the B-29 exclusively in the Pacific and Asian theaters. Allied leaders also decided to station two wings of B-29s in China, starting in February 1944. XX Bomber Command was activated on November 20, 1943, with orders to go to India, and from there to China.

That plan began falling apart almost immediately. The Chinese bases were originally to be in eastern China. Japanese offensives, launched due to rumors of the new long-range American bomber, captured territory intended for those bases. New bases deep in central China were built. Construction of the bases lagged behind schedule, as did B-29 development. February pushed into March without the B-29 becoming operational.

Even before the first B-29s headed towards China, a second front was planned. In March 1944, the decision was made to capture Saipan and Tinian, recapture Guam, and use these islands in the Marianas archipelago as B-29 bases. This would be the home of XXI Bomber Command, activated on March 1, 1944.

The first two parts of the grand strategy developed in 1942 were in motion by April 1944. The first wing of B-29s was heading towards China, and plans were made to build B-29 airbases in the Marianas after capturing those islands. What happened next underscored the axiom that no plan survives contact with the enemy.

Operations in China proved more difficult than anticipated, and less effective. Bases were primitive and logistics were difficult. The Fourteenth Air Force, tasked with protecting XX Bomber Command's bases, often failed. The B-29 airfield was in Chengdu, so far from Japan that B-29s could only reach western Kyushu. In November 1944, the B-29 bases in Saipan began launching missions against Japan. By that time the China-based B-29s had conducted only 18 missions, seven of which struck Japan.

This was despite giving command of XX Bomber Command in August 1944 to Major General Curtis LeMay, viewed as the Army Air Force's best heavy bomber leader. LeMay improved operational readiness, but quickly realized logistics made operating from China impractical. By December Chinese-based operations were being wound down.

The plan to liberate the Philippines approved in the summer of 1944 included recapture of Luzon. XXII Bomber Command was activated on August 14, 1944, with the intention of sending it to Luzon to supplement operations from the Marianas. This never happened. It was easier to expand Marianas operations or shift to Okinawa when that island became available. XXII Bomber Command remained in the United States and was disbanded in February 1945; XXIII Bomber Command was never activated.

The termination of China operations and the reluctance to commit resources to a Kurile Island invasion trimmed the four-prong attack into a single prong, operating from the Marianas. Eventually five, instead of the originally planned three wings were assigned to Marianas airfields as part of XXI Bomber Command.

All agreed the objective of the campaign was to destroy Japan's industry. Disagreement lay in the purpose of doing so. The Joint Chiefs of Staff viewed destruction of Japan's industry a precursor to invasion. Destroying industry reduced enemy ability to supply troops with weapons and munitions, especially artillery, armor, and most critically aircraft. A nation which lost the capability to produce equipment to replace combat losses quickly lost the ability to resist.

Air power advocates saw a greater opportunity. They believed that destroying a nation's industry, along with its transportation and energy distribution infrastructure, would compel surrender without a ground invasion.

Rarely can one man be said to be responsible for a campaign's success. Yet Curtis LeMay (pictured here while a brigadier general in China) turned around a faltering B-29 campaign. (LOC)

This radical vision, if approved, would make armies and navies obsolete, or at best subservient to strategic air power. They viewed the upcoming campaign as an opportunity to showcase strategic bombardment. These advocates opposed any diversion of B-29s or resources to support B-29s from any activity unrelated to strategic bombardment. This included mining missions or attacking Japanese airfields.

In its most extreme form, air power advocates opposed any use of B-29s for anything other than high-altitude daylight precision bombing (or perhaps for nighttime missions which employed precision radar-directed targeting, a different form of precision bombardment). Area bombing was viewed as indiscriminate, while medium- and low-altitude attacks failed to use the B-29's full capabilities.

The Kawasaki Ki-61 *Hein* (Allied code-name Tony) was the primary day fighter assigned to Home Island fighter squadrons. Its performance at high altitude was marginal, so one squadron adopted ramming tactics, stripping armament and armor to improve performance at altitude. (USNHHC)

The Army Air Force drew up target lists outlining different industries. Six were given priority: aircraft plants (including aircraft motors), petroleum refineries, iron and steel production, electronics, and antifriction bearings. Attacks were also urged against urban industrial areas vulnerable to incendiary attacks and merchant shipping in harbor and at sea.

Initial attacks from China struck iron and steel production. When the attackers switched to Marianas bases, priority shifted to the aircraft industry. Petroleum plants were reassigned lower priority as tankers were not reaching Japan and refineries were idle – they had nothing to refine. Precision bombing advocates awarded lowest priority to urban industrial areas and merchant shipping was outside the precision bombing paradigm. Incendiary raids were not precise and merchant shipping was hard to knock out with massed bombers.

Despite the Japanese transportation system's vulnerability to precision bombing, transport chokepoints were not targeted. Japanese railroads were running at capacity. Closing bridges, tunnels, and cuts would have crippled Japanese industry, yet these were ignored. Perhaps it was because these targets only required a B-29 group or squadron, not hundreds of aircraft. Or perhaps it was because they were most vulnerable to carrier-based dive bombers, which conceded a role to naval aviation.

By January 1945, after nine months, precision bombing had failed to deliver. High-altitude winds scattered bombs. The skies over Japan were frequently cloudy, making visual bombing impossible. Radar bombing accuracy, especially with under-trained operators using early-model ground target radar, proved imprecise. When everything aligned high-altitude precision bombing was devastating, but there were too few days where everything aligned over Japan to justify the investment in the B-29.

A new approach was tried. Best called the "just win" strategy, its proponents believed results mattered more than doctrine. Its chief proponent was Curtis LeMay, who had taken over command of XXI Bomber Command in January 1945. He viewed any use of the B-29

Medium-sized factories accounted for a significant percentage of Japan's industrial output. With light construction and high roofs they were vulnerable to both high explosives and incendiaries. (AC)

A Tokyo policeman in 1945. Civil defense should have played an important role protecting the workforce against air raids, but the Japanese government largely ignored it until B-29s began dropping bombs on Japan. (USNHHC)

that furthered Allied victory through strategic bombardment as permissible. LeMay realized that blocking Japanese waterways through B-29-deployed mines served a strategic bombing objective. Even if it helped the Navy, it denied Japanese industry badly needed raw materials and feedstock – and it could only be done with B-29s.

LeMay realized Japan's decentralized industry, with small subcontractors spread throughout crowded urban areas, was relatively immune to precision bombing, but appallingly exposed to area incendiary attack. If area incendiary attack was better performed at low or medium altitudes, LeMay believed it should be done at those altitudes at night, when Japanese antiaircraft defenses were weakest. When the weather permitted high-altitude daylight bombing, high-altitude daylight bombing should be done. When weather prevented precision visual bombing, conduct area incendiary raids.

In other words, LeMay supported doing anything that contributed to the objective of crippling Japanese industry. His approach was devastatingly effective.

Japanese defensive plans

Japan's objective in defending the homeland was straightforward: prevent aerial attacks on Japan. If attacked, repel the attackers. Japan's execution of plans to achieve these objectives was wretched, starting with failure at the grand strategic level.

Japan entered World War II with the goal of creating a ring of fortified positions at a distance so far from the Japanese Home Islands as to preclude air attack.

In 1941, before the Pacific stage of World War II started, except for Vladivostok and the Siberian territory around it, the nearest airfields from which a potential enemy could attack were in Luzon in the United States' Philippine Territory or the British Crown Colony of Hong Kong. Both were roughly 1,200 miles from Kyushu, beyond the range of a B-17. By the time the Japanese 1941–42 offensive ended, the nearest US airfield to Japan was on Midway Atoll, 2,500 miles away. For most of the war Japan, therefore, did not worry about home defense. The Doolittle Raid, when 16 land-based B-25s launched from an aircraft carrier attacked Japan, was embarrassing, but was recognized as a one-off stunt.

Even after Japanese intelligence began hearing rumors about the B-29 and the Very-Long Range program in early 1943, there was little concern about it. Japan still held its outer defense perimeter, an arc formed by Aleutians, Wake Island, the Gilbert and Caroline Islands,

New Ireland and New Britain, and New Guinea. The Allies had to reach either Luzon or the Marianas before the rumored super-bomber could reach Japan. To forestall the use of Chinese bases, the Imperial Japanese Army launched a land offensive intended to prevent them from being used to strike Japan. It succeeded to the extent that the one B-29 base constructed in China could only reach targets in southwest Kyushu.

It is hard to avoid concluding that Japan's home air defense plans were mired in wishful thinking. Even in 1944, when it became apparent the B-29 would be used, Japan remained in denial about the danger aerial bombardment posed to the Home Islands. In January the Japanese high command still seemed to act on the assumption that it remained impossible for the United States to capture the Marianas, and that operating B-29s out of China would prove too difficult. The issue of home defense would not arise – Japan would remain impossible for bombers to reach.

Part of this was the Japanese propensity to value the attack over the defense. Attack was everything. If you hit an opponent first, hard enough, that opponent would be out of the fight. Defense would thus be unnecessary. This approach worked well over the first six months of the war, when Japan seemed unstoppable. It had not completely worn out its validity by 1944. Air defense was still *defense*; therefore, it was given a lower priority.

There was no air defense in Japan before the Doolittle Raid. Thereafter, fighter units had been assigned to Japan, but little thought given to their use. Seventy fighters each were assigned to the three main industrial areas of Japan: Tokyo, Osaka-Kobe, and the Shimonoseki Strait area. These were drawn from two new fighter units and three training units converted to air defense units. In March 1944, this was expanded, slightly. The air brigade guarding Tokyo was increased to an air division, and an air brigade was formed to protect Nagoya.

Only after June 15, 1944 – when the United States launched its first B-29 strike (against Yawata) on the same day US troops landed at Saipan – did Japan overhaul its air defense structure. Eastern, Central, and Western District Armies were formed, headquartered respectively in Tokyo, Osaka, and Fukuoka. Each had an Army flying brigade with 85–90 fighters, and an assigned Navy air group, each with around 20 fighters. The Army could now request assistance from the Navy, but could not command the naval fighters. It was an improvement only in so far as the Army and Navy were at least talking to each other about air defense.

Over the next year improvements were made on the margins. The number of fighters was increased from 320 in July 1944 to 385 in February 1945. The Army's flying brigades covering Osaka and Fukuoka were upgraded to flying divisions and the Navy's air groups were increased to air flotillas. The number of aircraft assigned to these formations was increased only slightly, however. Worse, problems outlined in the infrastructure section remained. Aircraft stayed fixed geographically. Army and Navy cooperation remained minimal. Air operations rooms were established in each district army, but a complicated system of processing information within the centers ensured timely information never left. Fighters were not vectored towards the US formations. They had to waste time and fuel hunting the location of the enemy formations. Similarly, civil defense was never centralized. Each city organized its own civil defense, communications between cities were patchy, and civil defense best practices were not developed or distributed.

As if to concede the futility of Japan's air defense system, the one positive action taken by Japanese central planners was to disperse production facilities into the country and into caves. Scattering factories made them difficult targets for strategic bombardment, yet dispersal was not implemented until it was too late. Dispersal started in November 1944, after the first Marianas-based raids struck. The effort reduced overall production through to March 1945.

The principal reason for these shortcomings was the failure of Japan's planners. They failed to recognize the danger of a US strategic bombing campaign against Japan, failed to assign air defenses the resources needed to protect the homeland, and failed to use the resources they did have effectively.

THE CAMPAIGN
The B-29s go to war

Strategic bombing of Japan started on June 15, 1944. It ended exactly 14 months later, on August 15, 1945, when Imperial Japan surrendered to the Allied powers. The surrender was due in large part to the success of the strategic bombing campaign. It opened with 47 B-29s dropping bombs on Kyushu to little effect, but ended with over 800 B-29s leaving US bases on a single day, creating so much damage with conventional ordnance that the effects of two atomic bombs were dwarfed by them.

Over 14 months the United States built airbases to host both the attacking B-29 bombers and their escorting P-51 fighters, mounted a major air offensive against a determined foe, and defeated them. By its end, the United States owned the skies over Japan.

A line of bombers at Chengdu, China preparing to take off to bomb Yawata on June 15, 1944, the first strike against the Japanese homeland since the 1942 Doolittle Raid. Eleven war correspondents accompanied the mission. (USAAF)

An uncertain trumpet: June 15, 1944–January 20, 1945

On the night of June 15–16, the US Army Air Force XX Bomber Command opened the campaign of the strategic bombardment of Japan. On the afternoon of June 15, 1945 75 B-29s took off from Chengdu in China to attack the Imperial Iron and Steel Works at Yawata in Kyushu. The mission took the bombers to the limit of their range.

Each bomber carried eight 500lb general-purpose bombs, half their normal bomb load. Also aboard was every XX Bomber Command officer who could find an excuse to accompany the raid and ten war correspondents. Everyone wanted to participate in this historic first strike against Japan.

Because of fears of Japan's daytime air defenses, it was a nighttime mission, with the bombers flying over the target shortly after midnight. The aircraft did not fly in formation, reaching Yawata individually. It was intended as a precision strike, with the B-29s using radar to find the steel mill. The target was the coking ovens, which were fragile and difficult to rebuild.

Only 47 Superfortresses reached Japan, scattering bombs over northwest Kyushu. Only one bomb struck the steel works, hitting a power plant. Seven B-29s were lost, two possibly to enemy night fighters, the rest to accidents or post-mission attacks on Allied airfields by the Japanese.

The raid's most valuable outcome was revealing shortcomings in Japan's air defense over its Home Islands. Antiaircraft fire was heavy, but inaccurate. Radar interception was poor, and Japanese night fighters rarely found the B-29s. Allied planners absorbed these lessons.

On that same day, far east of Japan, Marines were storming ashore at Saipan, the first of three Marianas islands the United States would capture and convert into bases for B-29s.

The twin events shook Japan's leadership, causing the government led by Hideki Tojo to collapse. Its replacement intended to end the war, but was handicapped because it sought to surrender without admitting defeat – a task that ultimately proved impossible.

The Yawata raid was not the first combat mission flown by the B-29s in the Far East. That honor fell to 98 B-29s launched from Allied bases in India on June 5, sent on a daylight attack to Bangkok, Thailand. Between June 5 and mid-November 1944, XX Bomber Command averaged one major mission every two weeks.

Most were against targets on the Asian mainland, Formosa, or the Dutch East Indies. Only six more struck Japan. XX Bomber Command next visited Japan on the evening of July 7–8. Another night raid, it involved only 18 bombers and attacked targets in southwestern Kyushu: Sasabo, Omura, and Tobata. This was followed up by a 29-plane night raid on Nagasaki.

On August 20, 1944, XX Bomber Command launched its first daylight raid against Japan. The target was again Yawata, with 98 B-29s scheduled to leave Chengdu. After 75 took off, a B-29 crashed on takeoff, preventing the remaining aircraft from launching until the wreck was cleared. The first 74 pressed on to launch a daylight strike, while 13 others attacked at night.

The daylight bombers went in at 25,000ft. Sixty-one planes made it to the target, six others hitting alternate targets. Flak over Yawata was intense, but only knocked down one B-29 (eight others were damaged). *Hein* fighters attacked the formation, but only downed three Superfortresses: one B-29 was destroyed through gunfire, a second was rammed, probably deliberately, and another was hit by flying debris from the collision and went down. Besides the combat losses, ten other B-29s were lost to accidents and mechanical failures, including one which crashed prior to the mission, staging from India.

The raid's effects were minor. Two coking ovens were thought damaged for three to six months, with other plant installations believed damaged. The mission's most important result was again revealing that Japanese air defenses were less formidable than previously believed. Antiaircraft fire, even in daylight, was ineffectual. Japanese fighters, even against unescorted B-29s, were little more effective, being barely able to reach the bombers. Ramming proved the most successful tactic against the bomber.

The low productivity of XX Bomber Command led to a change in leadership. On August 29, Curtis LeMay took charge. He overhauled operations, maintenance, and training. He changed the B-29 formations from sets of four-plane diamonds to the 12-aircraft box used in Europe. He also instituted a system of lead crews and formation bombing, as well as flying a larger percentage of daylight missions. LeMay led by example, flying as an observer on the first B-29 mission after his arrival, a September 8 raid sending 108 B-29s against the Showa Iron Works in Anshan, Manchuko.

While LeMay improved readiness and performance, logistical obstacles and geography prevented expanding the Chengdu operation. In the first 60 days after LeMay took over, eight missions were flown (including three with over 100 aircraft launched). Only one – a high-altitude daytime strike against Omura – hit Japan. The Omura mission saw 59 bombers out of 78 sortied drop general-purpose bombs and incendiaries. Two more missions struck the aircraft factory at Omura in November 1944 without doing significant damage.

After that, mainland China operations began winding down. The bases in the Marianas were operational by October 1944. The first B-29 landed at Saipan on October 12,

piloted by the commander of XXI Bomber Command, Brigadier General Haywood S. "Possum" Hansell, Jr. Difficulty operating in China and India led air commanders in Washington to close things down there, and operating B-29s exclusively from bases in the Central Pacific. Two more missions against Omura launched from Chengdu, one in December 1944 and another in January 1945. Neither did much damage. Most of the remaining raids were launched against Formosa or mainland Asian targets. The last was flown in March 1945.

Starting operations on Saipan proved as frustrating as getting things started in China. Superfortresses trickled into Saipan throughout October and into November. By November 15, of the 73rd Bomb Wing's (the first operational B-29 wing at Saipan) authorized strength of 180 Superfortresses, only 90 had arrived.

Combat missions started in October, when 18 B-29s were sent on a training mission to Truk. Hansell accompanied that mission, but was aboard one of the four B-29s that aborted due to mechanical issues. Fourteen bombers reached the neutralized Japanese bastion, dropped bombs on submarine pens, faced light flak, and saw one Zero (which prudently stayed out of range). Three more missions were flown against Truk and two against airfields on Japanese-held Iwo Jima through to November 21. While no casualties had resulted, bombing results were dismal. Crews needed more training.

Regardless, the XXI was sent to bomb Japan. F-13s, the photo-reconnaissance Superfortresses, had been flying photographic missions since November 1, gathering targeting intelligence. "Hap" Arnold wanted the first mission to hit Tokyo with at least 100 B-29s. This raid was originally scheduled for November 17, but weather delayed the strike until the 24th. The target was Nakajima's Musashino aircraft factory on Tokyo's outskirts; 111 B-29s took off.

XXI Bomber Command intelligence expected a hot reception. It estimated 400–500 fighters guarding Tokyo (rather than the 370-odd fighters guarding the entire country). To distract attention from Tokyo, nine F-13s were sent to Nagoya, where they dropped "rope" to create the illusion of a massive bomber formation attacking that city, and split Japanese air defenses. Thought was given to radar jamming, but little was known about Japanese radar at that stage. It was feared jamming might reveal too much about US ECM capabilities. Therefore jamming was not used.

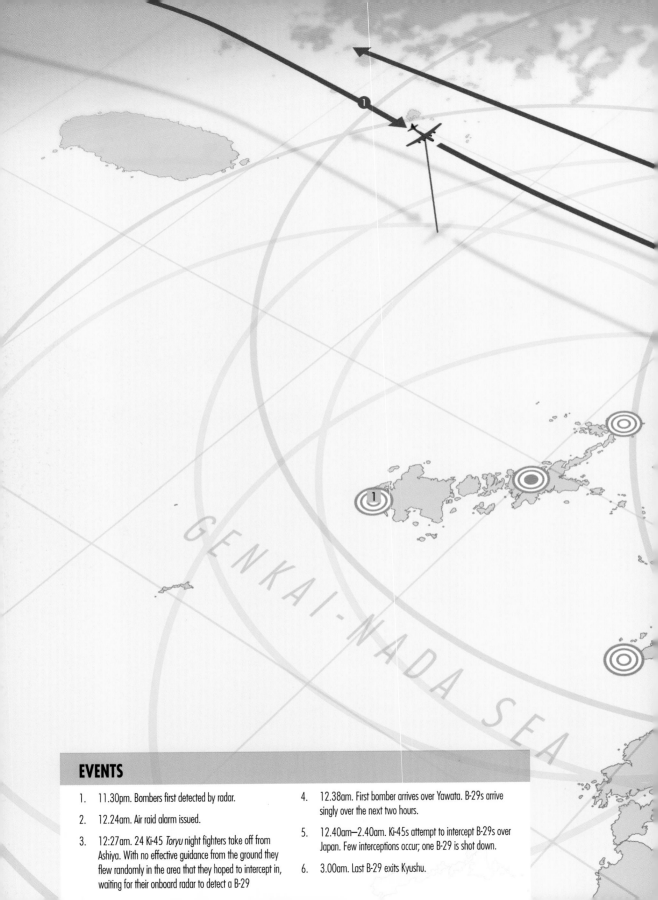

GENKAI-NADA SEA

EVENTS

1. 11.30pm. Bombers first detected by radar.

2. 12.24am. Air raid alarm issued.

3. 12:27am. 24 Ki-45 *Toryu* night fighters take off from Ashiya. With no effective guidance from the ground they flew randomly in the area that they hoped to intercept in, waiting for their onboard radar to detect a B-29

4. 12.38am. First bomber arrives over Yawata. B-29s arrive singly over the next two hours.

5. 12.40am–2.40am. Ki-45s attempt to intercept B-29s over Japan. Few interceptions occur; one B-29 is shot down.

6. 3.00am. Last B-29 exits Kyushu.

First strike at Japan: the Yawata raid

June 15–16, 1944

Just after midnight 47 B-29s from the Twentieth Air Force bombed the Yawata Steel Works in Northwestern Kyushu – the first air strike against Japan's Home Islands since the 1942 Doolittle Raid. The Superfortresses flew a round-trip distance of over 3200 miles from bases in Chengdu, China.

USAAF units ●
1. 58th Bombardment Wing

IJAAF Units ●
1. 4th Air Regiment
2. 59th Air Regiment

Commanding the 73rd Bombardment Wing against Japan was Brigadier General Emmett "Rosey" O'Donnell. Shown briefing crews before a mission to Japan, O'Donnell personally led the first mission to Tokyo and the March 9–10 incendiary raid. (AC)

Of the 111 bombers sent to Tokyo, only 24 hit the Musashino factory. Seventeen aborted before reaching Japan, six were unable to bomb, and 64 dropped bombs on targets of opportunity, such as the docks and Tokyo's urban area.

Antiaircraft fire was generally inaccurate. Only one B-29 was lost to enemy action, deliberately rammed by a damaged *Hein*. Intelligence officers estimated the bombers had been attacked by 125 fighters – an overestimation, because only 70-odd fighters were in the Tokyo area. One B-29 ran out of gasoline and ditched, eight were damaged by enemy action, and three by friendly fire.

The raid caused as little damage to the Japanese as the Japanese did to the B-29s. Of the 240 500lb bombs dropped on the Musashino factory only 48 (including three duds) landed inside the compound. Yet the raid revealed the impotence of Japan's air defense system, while demonstrating to the six million people living in Tokyo that they could be hit with impunity.

The mission set the pattern for the next three months. XXI Bomber Command struck at Japan with a series of high-altitude daylight precision attacks that did little damage to their targets, but resulted in light combat losses. The 73rd Bomb Wing revisited Musashino four times more: on November 27, December 3, December 22, and December 27. It also launched high-altitude raids against aircraft factories in Nagoya on December 13 and 18. None were successful: clouds obscured the targets or winds scattered the bombs.

Over his objections and at the direct orders of Arnold, Hansell conducted three incendiary missions. One, a night raid against Tokyo with 29 bombers on November 29–30, started fires that were contained after burning the equivalent of 27 city blocks. Daylight incendiary raids were made against Nagoya on December 21, 1944 and January 3, 1945, with 78 and 97 aircraft respectively. These also failed to start conflagrations, partly because when dropped from 25,000 to 33,000ft the incendiaries scattered too widely. Meanwhile, LeMay and XX Bomber Command had launched a devastatingly successful fire raid against Hanchow in China on December 18.

Japan was proving as unsuccessful in stopping the B-29s as the B-29s were in bombing Japan. Total bomber losses remained low, averaging just 4.4 percent per mission. Most losses were related to fuel management, with crews running out of gasoline returning home. The Japanese were more successful when they struck the bombers at their bases. They launched a series of raids against Saipan using bombers staging at Iwo Jima. Two raids destroyed four B-29s, seriously damaged six more and hit 22 other Superfortresses. XXI Bomber Command retaliated with strikes against Japan's Iwo Jima airfields, aided by carrier aircraft.

By December, Arnold was concerned about the lack of results from XXI Bomber Command. The United States' most expensive weapons program was not delivering results. Curtis LeMay had turned around XX Bomber Command, and was slated to take over XXII Bomber Command in the Philippines. But unless the B-29 proved itself, soon, there would be no XXII Bomber Command. Arnold decided to promote LeMay over Hansell. LeMay was given command of all B-29s in the field and told to run the show from the

Marianas. Hansell was informed of the change on January 6. LeMay asked Hansell to stay, but Hansell opted to leave. LeMay took over XXI Bomber Command on January 20.

The last raid planned by Hansell was made on January 19 against the Kawasaki Aircraft Industries Company at Akashi. In 1944 the plant delivered one-sixth of Japan's airframes and one-eighth of its engines. Another precision raid with 62 B-29s dumped 620 bombs on the plant. Every important building was hit and production was cut by 90 percent.

The first round: January 20–March 18

LeMay's operations during his first six weeks in command of the Marianas-based B-29s were similar to those of General Hansell. Most were high-altitude daytime strikes. LeMay did have more aircraft: by January a second wing, the 313th Bombardment Wing was operational, flying out of Tinian. Bombing results remained unchanged through January and February: miserable. On one mission against the Nakajima aircraft factory in Ota, 14 percent of the bombs landed on the target. Of those that hit, nearly half of the 500lb bombs were duds. Nearly one-third of the factory buildings were damaged, but most of the damage was done by incendiaries mixed with the high-explosive bombs. (The plant produced the Ki-84 *Hayate*, of which the raid destroyed 74.)

LeMay experimented with incendiaries. On February 3, 129 B-29s from both the 73rd and 313th visited Kobe with a mixed load of incendiaries and fragmentation bombs. (One-twelfth of the load was fragmentation bombs.) Results were encouraging: 60 acres of the industrial southwest portion of Kobe burned. This and the Ota strike were suggestive of the way forward.

A February 25 strike at Tokyo dispatched 192 B-29s, testing incendiaries. Each B-29 carried one 500lb bomb and 4,500lb of incendiaries. The raid burned out a square mile of Tokyo. That mission, along with a precision strike against the Musashino factory on February 19, was made to indirectly support the invasion of Iwo Jima, which occurred on the same day.

What was discouraging were US losses. Japan overhauled its air defenses in late December 1944, revamping civil defense organizations within cities, dispersing critical production, and beefing up fighter defenses. The last took a toll on US forces. Losses jumped in January and February to 5.7 percent of the bombers over target. On the Kobe strike one B-29 was shot down by fighters and 35 others damaged. At Ota, 12 B-29s were shot down and 29 damaged. February losses totaled 75 bombers: 29 to fighters, one to antiaircraft fire,

The round trip from the Marianas to Japan and back was over 3,200 miles: 12 hours of flying over mostly open ocean. Here a B-29 comes in for a sunset landing at Guam after a long daylight mission to Japan. (AC)

nine to fighters and flak, 21 to operational difficulties (typically fuel or mechanical failure), and 15 to causes unknown.

As March began, LeMay realized high-level precision bombing was not going to subdue Japan. It was not working. Clouds obscured visual sighting of targets and bombardiers proved unable to reliably find the target with requisite accuracy. Radar bombing was disappointing because ground-tracking radar barely had the resolution needed for precision bombing and radar operators lacked the skill and experience to obtain that accuracy.

Bombardiers and radar operators were good enough to support area bombing, using incendiaries. The B-29's best defense against Japan's most deadly bomber-killer, fighter aircraft, was high altitude, but if the bombers dropped incendiaries from high altitude, the incendiaries scattered too much to get fire density sufficient to overwhelm firefighting efforts and allow fires to spread. Daytime raids at 10,000–14,000ft, the best height for incendiaries, would raise fighter losses to unacceptable levels.

On March 4, LeMay ordered a daytime precision strike on Musashino, the seventh raid. The 192 bombers sent arrived to find the target clouded over. In 20 missions precision bombing had done minimal damage. Japanese aircraft production was disrupted more by Japanese industry dispersion than by bombing. On March 6, a frustrated LeMay told his public relations officer: "This outfit has been getting a lot of publicity without having really accomplished a hell of a lot in bombing results." LeMay decided to change tactics.

On March 9, crews got a preflight briefing for a mission unlike any previously flown. The target was Tokyo. It was to be a maximum effort: 334 B-29s from three different wings would be sent. The bombers were to strike at night, the first planes arriving shortly after midnight. The aircraft would not fly in formation, but proceed individually to the target. They were also scheduled to fly at altitudes between 5,000 and 10,000ft.

The bomb load was unusually heavy: 16,000lb per aircraft exclusively composed of incendiary bombs. This was possible for two reasons. First, significantly less fuel was required. Eliminating formation flying meant pilots did not need to waste fuel to stay rigidly aligned with the other aircraft in the formation. Low altitude eliminated the fuel required to climb to 30,000ft. The second reason seemed more ominous to aircrew. To gain payload, LeMay was sending the aircraft in without ammunition, except for bottom turrets. Those were to be used to shoot out searchlights.

Crews viewed the plan as a suicide mission. They believed low altitude would make them easy targets for Japanese antiaircraft fire. Without bullets for defensive guns they could not fight off their most feared enemy, Japanese fighters. The commander picked to lead the mission objected to the plan because of the perceived risk to his crews.

LeMay's calculation was simple. Japanese night fighter capability was so bad it could be ignored, so carrying ammunition to fight them was unnecessary. Japanese early-warning radar did not report the altitude of attacking aircraft. Japanese antiaircraft guns fused shells to explode at specific altitudes and initially set them for the expected altitudes of between 25,000 and 32,000ft. Until antiaircraft gunners re-set their shells the early-arriving aircraft would be missed. If large enough fires were set, gunners would be too busy surviving to shoot at late-arriving aircraft. Intelligence also indicated that few medium antiaircraft guns defended Tokyo. Medium antiaircraft guns, ineffective against high-altitude B-29s, were assigned where medium-level bombing occurred.

At 6.15pm local time the first B-29s took off from Saipan. They were joined by aircraft from Tinian and Guam. By 7.17pm 325 B-29s were airborne. Crews with the best pilots and most experienced navigators and bombardiers were assigned to the leading aircraft. These aircraft were armed with 180 M-47 bombs, intended to start fires requiring motorized firefighting equipment. The objective was the Asakusa district, the most crowded section of Tokyo, with the highest population density. It contained large numbers of small machine shops producing subcontracted parts for larger factories. Asakusa was easy to find on radar thanks to a series of rivers running through it.

The pathfinder B-29s arrived shortly after 1.00am in Tokyo and carved a flaming "X" across the district with their M-47s, marking the target. Follow-on bombers were armed with 24 clusters of M-69 incendiaries. The leading aircraft had the clusters open at 2,000ft. Follow-on aircraft had clusters fused to open at 2,500ft for a dense distribution of the small incendiaries. Each cluster would scatter M-69s across a 500ft by 2,500ft area. The M-47s were set to ignite at 100ft; the M-69s at 50ft.

The raid succeeded beyond planners' most optimistic predictions. Incendiaries caused enough fires to overwhelm the firefighters. Small fires merged into large fires. The wind

Many components used to assemble aircraft and weapons by Japan's large factories were made by subcontractors in home industry machine shops. They were interspersed throughout crowded and combustible residential districts, with workers living above their workplaces. (AC)

Operation *Meetinghouse*

March 9/10, 1945

In March 1945 General Curtis LeMay changed American bombing tactics dramatically. Instead of depending on high-level precision daylight bombing he decided to experiment with mass incendiary attacks at low levels conducted at night. The first was made against Tokyo on the night of March 9/10. The raid, Operation *Meetinghouse*, was devastatingly effective.

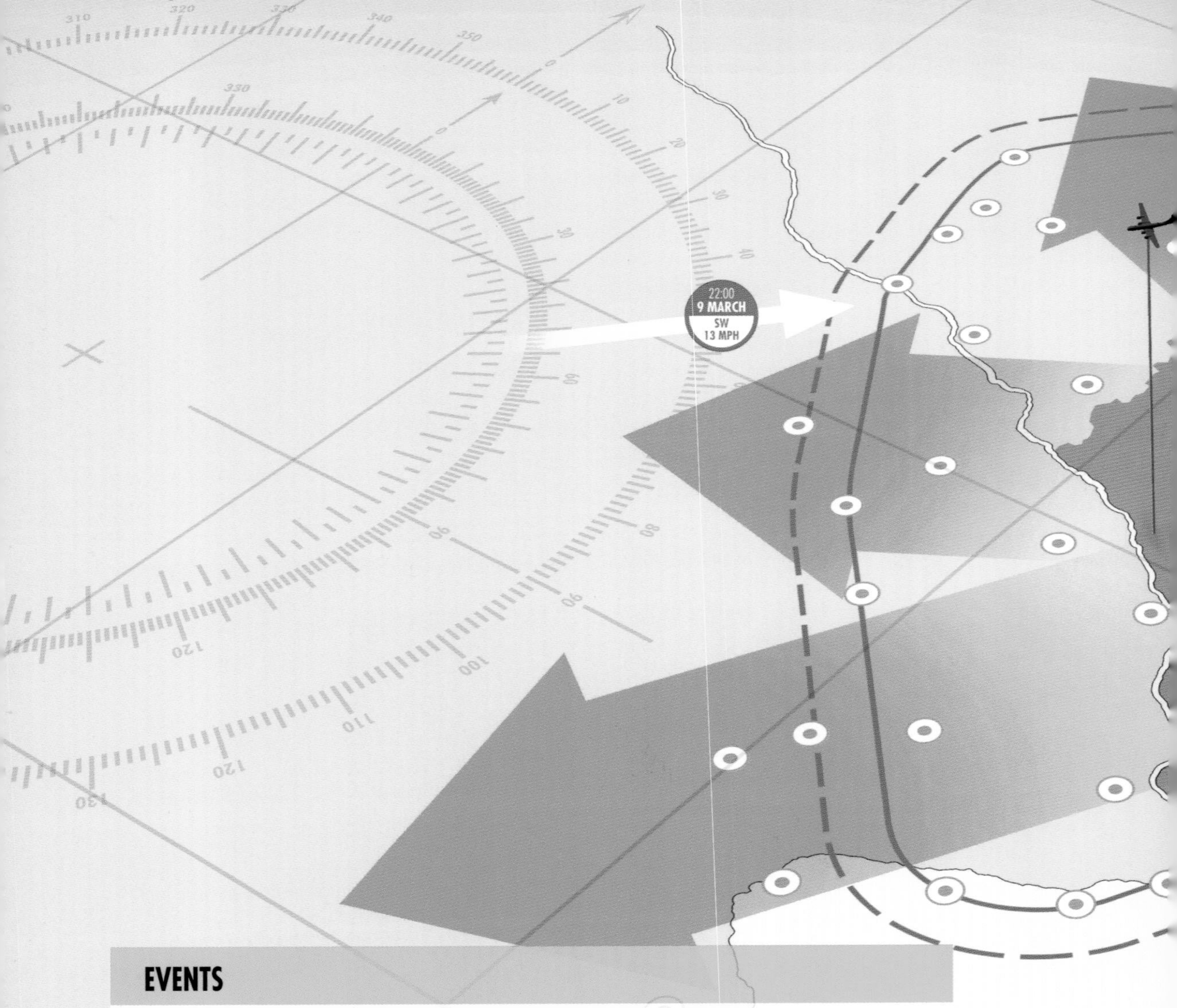

24:00 9 MARCH W 9 MPH

22:00 9 MARCH SW 13 MPH

EVENTS

1. At 1.21am Pathfinders strike aiming points with M-47 incendiaries

2. 73rd Wing follows a heading between 290 and 309 degrees over the target area

3. 313th Wing follows a heading of 305 degrees over the target area

4. 314th Wing follows a heading between 210 and 240 degrees over the target area.

5. By 3.30am fires are widespread throughout the target area.

6. Fires are started outside target area due to poor targeting or a desire to drop bombs quickly

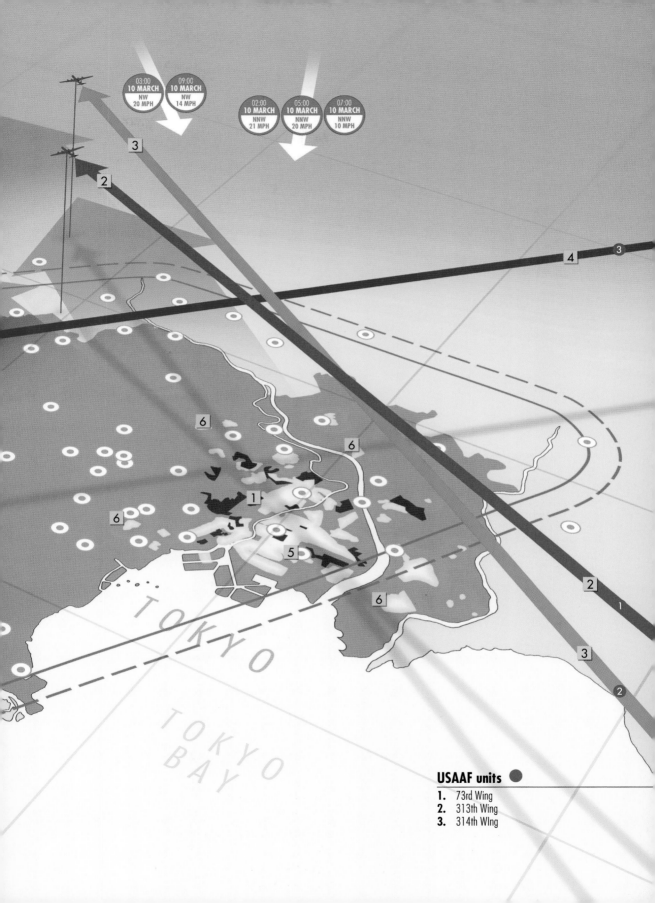

03:00
10 MARCH
NW
20 MPH

09:00
10 MARCH
NW
14 MPH

02:00
10 MARCH
NNW
21 MPH

05:00
10 MARCH
NNW
20 MPH

07:00
10 MARCH
NNW
10 MPH

3

2

4

3

6

6

6

6

1

5

2

3

2

1

TOKYO

TOKYO

BAY

USAAF units ●

1. 73rd Wing
2. 313th Wing
3. 314th WIng

The March 9–10 fire raid used a mixture of M-47 and M-69 incendiaries. The M-69s were packaged in E-46 aimable cluster packages. Here ordnance men load E-46 clusters into the bomb bay of a B-29. (AC)

picked up to 21mph after 2.00am, creating a wave firestorm. Late-arriving bombers reported the skies over Tokyo as bright as daytime. Updrafts tossed the B-29s as if they were paper airplanes. Fires were so intense they consumed all oxygen, suffocating anyone in bomb shelters.

The fires burned until well after sunrise. When they finally burned out, almost 16 square miles of Tokyo, containing over a quarter of a million buildings, was ashes. Many of Tokyo's fire engines had been destroyed, caught in the firestorm. Casualty counts ranged between 83,000 and 150,000 dead. It was the deadliest air raid of the war. Output from the Musashino aircraft factory, largely undamaged by eight daylight precision raids, dropped. The plant had not been damaged, but the raid had burned out many subcontractors providing the factory with parts.

Nine B-29s were lost as a result of enemy air defenses, with 42 damaged. Four other aircraft were lost to non-combat causes. The losses were lower than during the daylight missions and the results spectacularly better.

Two days later, on March 11, a second night incendiary raid was mounted. The target was Nagoya, Japan's third largest city and the heart of its aircraft industry. This time 313 planes took off and 285 bombed the city. The bombers carried 200 rounds of .50-caliber ammunition in the tail guns. A mix of M-47 and M-69 incendiaries was again used as there were insufficient stocks of M-47s to use those exclusively. Nearly 40 fires started, but they did not spread; there was no wind, and Nagoya had well-spaced firebreaks and adequate water. Only just over 2 square miles was burned, and the aircraft plants not seriously hurt. Only one B-29 was lost (ditching after takeoff) and 20 damaged.

Osaka, Japan's second largest city, was hit next. A major industrial target, Osaka's arsenal produced one-fifth of the Imperial Army's ammunition. It was also an important shipbuilding and electrical-equipment manufacturing center.

Of 301 bombers which took off late in the afternoon of March 13, 274 reached Osaka. Due to the greater range and more ammunition carried, the Superfortresses carried only 12,000lb of incendiaries. Cloud cover forced bombers to use radar bombing, yet ironically, this provided better results than the visual targeting. A more uniform distribution of incendiaries resulted. Fires spread and burned out just over 8 square miles of the city. The commercial district was flattened, 119 important factories in the industrial district were destroyed, and nearly 135,000 buildings burned down. US losses were again light: only two B-29s were lost (one in combat) and 13 damaged.

XXI Bomber Command was back over Japan on March 16, sending 307 B-29s to Kobe, the country's sixth largest city and most important overseas port. By this time, M-47 and M-69 incendiaries were running low. Most of the 2,355 tons dropped on Kobe were M-17A1s. These were 500lb clusters of 4lb magnesium-thermite incendiaries. They were better against factories and other reinforced structures, but not as effective as the napalm incendiaries against wooden buildings.

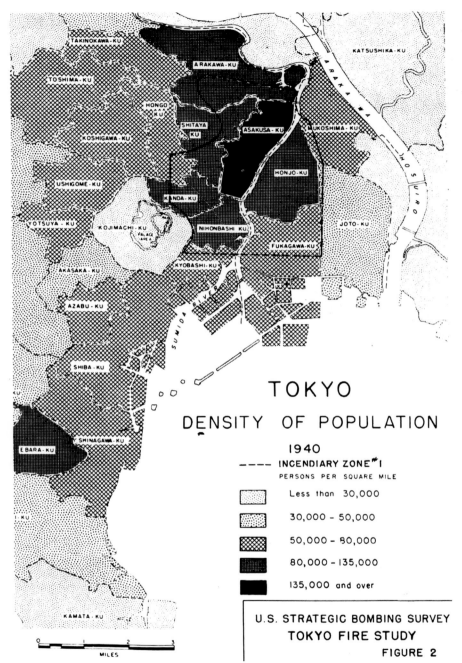

TOKYO

DENSITY OF POPULATION

1940

- - - - INCENDIARY ZONE *1

PERSONS PER SQUARE MILE

Less than 30,000

30,000 - 50,000

50,000 - 80,000

80,000 - 135,000

135,000 and over

U.S. STRATEGIC BOMBING SURVEY
TOKYO FIRE STUDY
FIGURE 2

MILES

Fires spread over the southeastern industrial district and the business district. The Kawasaki shipyards were heavily damaged. Five hundred industrial buildings were burned out, 66,000 homes destroyed, and nearly 3 square miles of Kobe – 20 percent of its area – burned. Just three bombers were lost.

On March 19 the B-29s returned to Nagoya. Every third bomber carried two 500lb general-purpose bombs. The rest of the load contained whatever incendiaries remained in the ordnance stores. The high-explosive bombs were intended to disrupt firefighting.

XXI Bomber Command could only mount five maximum-effort missions in ten days through unrelenting effort on the part of maintenance staff. They worked around the clock to repair damaged aircraft and refit worn ones. (USAAF)

A total of 313 B-29s were sent, 290 arrived, and 1,858 tons of bombs, high-explosive, and incendiary struck Nagoya.

The results were better than the last Nagoya raid, but worse than any of the other fire-raids. Only 3 square miles was burned out. Serious damage was done to the freight yards, the Aichi engine factory, and the Nagoya arsenal. Lack of success was relative: this raid was deadlier than any other prior to March 9.

A return to precision bombing: March 20–April 15

The Nagoya raid closed the ten-day incendiary campaign. It was not because it was unsuccessful. In just over a week LeMay found how to turn the B-29 into an industry-destroying weapon. Every one of the five raids did more damage to Japan's industries than the entire bombing campaign against Japan from June 15, 1944 to March 4, 1945. Losses had been low; Japan proved unable to stop the attacks.

Civilian casualties in the final four raids of the ten-day fire blitz were much smaller than the Tokyo raid. Nearly 100,000 died in the Tokyo raid; deaths in the next four raids were less than 10,000 in each. Part of the reason was better preparedness on the part of the Japanese. The three precursor incendiary attacks had caused Japanese civil defense authorities to grossly underestimate the destructive potential of fire raids against urban areas.

Japan's air defense command realized it was in trouble. Japan struggled to cope with high-altitude daylight attacks. Fighters had difficulty intercepting due to the altitude and speed of the US bombers. It took fighters 15 minutes to climb to the altitudes at which the B-29s flew. The Army's radar system gave about 25 minutes warning of an incoming raid. (The Navy, thanks to a radar station on Hachijo, had an hour's warning of a raid heading towards Tokyo. Frequently it did not pass warnings to the Army, especially initially.)

At the speeds B-29s flew, the lead aircraft reached Tokyo only 40 minutes after the bombers were spotted on radar. Fighters at the primary interceptor bases guarding Tokyo barely had time to take off, get to altitude, find the bomber formation, and attack it before formations reached Tokyo, bombed, and headed home.

Japan's air defense had more time to react if the targets were further inland, such as Nagoya, Osaka, and Kobe, but it lacked the fighter strength necessary to meet the daylight raids. With 70 to 100 fighters per region, fighters were often outnumbered by bombers, especially when the United States started sending 125 or more bombers on a strike.

In April Japan increased fighter strength by 20 percent, raising its national total to 450. Yet fighters remained assigned geographically. The diversion conducted against Nagoya during the first Tokyo raid did not reduce the fighter strength Japan sent against the Tokyo-bound bombers, as Nagoya and Tokyo were in different Army areas guarded by different fighter units.

Up until the first fire blitz, Japan's leaders could take comfort from knowing US daytime bombing had been largely ineffectual. With the new tactic of nighttime area bombing, the Americans had found an effective way to attack Japan.

The Japanese could not readily counter these night attacks. Their daytime fighters were barely able to deal with B-29s; the night fighters were proving totally ineffectual. By changing altitude, LeMay made it more difficult for the Japanese to predict the height of the B-29s. On the March 9–10 Tokyo raid, the night fighters were seeking the bombers at the expected altitudes of between 28,000 and 32,000ft, while the bombers – with empty machine guns – snuck in tens of thousands of feet lower.

Japan needed to radically overhaul its air defense system. Instead leaders made a few minor, largely cosmetic, changes. Rather than integrating Army and Navy resources, the high command urged greater cooperation. They kept air defense commands regional and failed to develop ground-based fighter direction systems that Great Britain, Germany, and the United States all successfully used – in the case of Great Britain, since before the Battle of Britain in 1940.

The March 13–14 incendiary attack on Osaka burned out over 8 square miles, gutting the commercial district and completely destroying 134,744 houses. (LOC)

Firefighters in Tokyo: March 10, 1945

On March 9–10, 1945, General Curtis LeMay launch his unprecedented and first low-level mass firebombing raid against Japan, sending 300 B-29s to burn out the heart of Tokyo.

The target was Tokyo's Asakusa district, one of the most densely populated places in the world in 1945. It was also one of the most densely built-up, filled with flammable one- and two-story wooden buildings, a perfect target for an incendiary raid. What started as a few separate fires soon grew into a wave firestorm as more and more aircraft dropped incendiaries into the periphery of the already burning area.

This plate shows the raid from the point of view of the firefighters' attempt to fight the blaze. The scene is just south of the Matsuya department store, a major Asakusa district landmark. The Asakusa railroad station was in the basement of this building. It is after midnight, perhaps 1.00am Tokyo time. The fire has gained enough strength to begin overwhelming the Tokyo Fire Department. Three sets of firefighters can be seen. Two are with the 500-gallon-per-minute pumper trucks then standard in Japan. Another group of firefighters is operating a hand-drawn 120-gallon-per-minute motor-operated pump.

These firefighters are lucky enough to be next to the Sumida River. They can draw water from the river by trailing their hoses into the river off the Azuma Bridge, which gives them an unlimited supply of water. Unfortunately, there is not enough water to contain the fires. The low single-story shops along the street are fully engulfed with flames. So is the low-rise office building down the street and virtually everything else.

The Matsuya department store, a sturdy building of reinforced concrete, was used by Tokyo residents as a bomb shelter during this raid. The flames grew so intense that they consumed all of the oxygen in the building. While the building survived the raid (and remains a Tokyo landmark today), no one inside did.

As for the firefighters, the fires are gaining ground and growing uncontrollably. The firemen will soon have to make a choice: flee or die.

The US paused the incendiary campaign due to its success: XXI Bomber Command had burned through the stockpiles of incendiaries in the Marianas. Planners assumed B-29s would carry 4-ton loads, with each wing flying 735 sorties per month. They also assumed incendiaries would be 40 percent of the tonnage. That meant a stockpile of 3,600 tons of incendiaries was adequate. However, the five-mission campaign consisted of 1,559 sorties and consumed 3,900 tons of incendiaries.

One lesson from the eight incendiary raids conducted was the need to overwhelm the capacity of the firefighters. The three test incendiary raids failed to reach critical density. The March 9–10 Tokyo raid and March 13–14 Osaka raid showed what happened when density of fires overwhelmed firefighting. LeMay would not order more fire raids until he had sufficient stocks of incendiaries to replicate previous results. Logistics thus drove the offensive. XXI Bomber Command stood down for a few days to repair damage and overhaul equipment.

LeMay was unwilling to let the B-29s stand idle. He tried another experiment: nighttime precision bombing. If successful it would exploit Japan's weak night defenses and allow XXI Bomber Command to use existing stocks of general-purpose bombs. On March 24, 248 B-29s took off for Nagoya. The target was the Mitsubishi engine plant.

The attack started with ten B-29s dropping flares to light up the factory. Five minutes later ten more B-29s, pathfinders, would drop M-17 incendiary clusters to mark the target with flame. The remaining bombers armed with 500lb GP bombs would drop their bombs into the flames.

The plan went awry as soon as the bombers arrived. Thick cloud cover blanketed the factory and some incendiaries went astray. Smoke obscured the lights from the incendiaries that did hit the factory. Of 1,500 tons of bombs dropped, only 60 tons fell inside the factory, causing negligible damage.

The Japanese Army's first-line night fighter, the Kawasaki Ki-45 *Toryu*, proved almost completely unable to stop night-bombing B-29s. During the first Tokyo raid the fighters waited for B-29s at high altitude, while the bombers attacked underneath them. (AC)

Since a multi-wing raid did not work, LeMay allowed his wing commanders to experiment with precision night tactics individually. On March 30–April 1, the 314th Wing sent 14 B-29s to Mitsubishi's Nagoya aircraft engine factory. Twelve bombed the target, illuminated by flares, but missed entirely. The following day the 73rd sent 121 B-29s on a night raid to the Nakajima Musashi aircraft plant. Again flares were used to illuminate the target for night precision bombing. Only 16 500lb bombs of the 1,000 tons dropped fell inside the perimeter, causing little damage.

On the night of April 3, LeMay sent in three wings against Nagoya independently: one each against the Mitsubishi and Tachikawa aircraft engine plants and the Nakajima Koizumi aircraft assembly plant. The results were identical to previous attempts: negligible damage.

Starting on April 7, P-51s from Iwo Jima began escorting B-29s, allowing LeMay to resume daylight missions. Superfortresses could also now fly at lower altitudes. The bombers no longer had to fly above the Japanese fighters' performance window. Precision nighttime bombing was suddenly unimportant.

XXI Bomber Command also decided to unleash its ECM capabilities on April 7. Each B-29 squadron carried 12 airborne jamming transmitters. These blocked Japanese searchlight-control and gunnery-control radar. ECM transmitters had been on B-29s since the Marianas-based bombing of Japan started in November 1944, but XXI Bomber Command had previously hesitated to use these electronics. It feared their use would provide Japan with critical information about US ECM capabilities, allowing the Japanese to develop countermeasures. By March, XXI Bomber Command intelligence was familiar with Japanese radar capabilities and decided Japan lacked the infrastructure to block jamming.

Fighter squadrons operating from airstrips on Iwo Jima flew their first escort mission on April 7, 1945. From then on, weather permitting, daytime missions were escorted by P-51 Mustangs, making it more difficult for Japanese interceptors to attack the bombers. (NMUSAF)

Jammers, used for the first time on April 7, provided a huge advantage. Centralized antiaircraft gun control was blinded. Individual batteries reverted to local control, aiming guns visually. The quality of gunners varied widely, and the best-trained personnel were at the now-useless gunnery-control radars. The effectiveness of the flak batteries, marginal under the best conditions above 20,000ft, became virtually useless.

Over 150 bombers from the 313th and 314th Bombardment Wings flew over Mitsubishi's Nagoya engine works at 20,500ft. The daylight skies were clear. The target was flattened, the plant losing 90 percent of its capacity. The 73rd Wing hit the oft-missed Tokyo Musashi aircraft factory with 101 B-29s, loaded with 2,000lb bombs. The big bombs damaged machine shops and knocked down 10 percent of the other buildings.

A follow-up raid on April 12 sent 112 B-29s, again with 2,000lb bombs to destroy heavy machinery. This mission had heavy haze, requiring radar bombing. This finished off the Musashi plant. Eleven B-29s which failed to find Musashi bombed the alternate target – the brand-new Mitsubishi Shizuoka aircraft engine factory. It was flattened, 86 percent of the roof area was destroyed. P-51s stymied Japanese fighters; interceptors damaged 36 Superfortresses, but shot down none.

LeMay attempted to lure the fighters away from Tokyo by attacking Koriyama, 120 miles north of the capital, with over 130 aircraft. The diversion failed because the fighters were restricted geographically. The attack itself was successful, bombers from the 313th and 314th Wings destroying two chemical plants producing tetraethyl-lead (used in high-octane gasoline) and an aluminum plant. If Japan was refining aviation gasoline at maximum capacity, the raid would have caused a dramatic drop in aviation fuel. But Japan was getting little crude oil; its refineries were virtually closed.

The incendiary shortage was over as well by mid-April, allowing resumption of nighttime area bombing. Even though daytime precision bombing was now working, the March fire raids had been even more effective. LeMay revisited Tokyo. The metropolitan area was struck by 327 B-29s on the night of April 13–14. This time the target was the arsenal district, northwest of the Imperial Palace compound. The district was filled with factories manufacturing and warehouses storing small arms, artillery, munitions, explosives and gunpowder, and weapons-focused electronics and machinery, such as gunnery-control

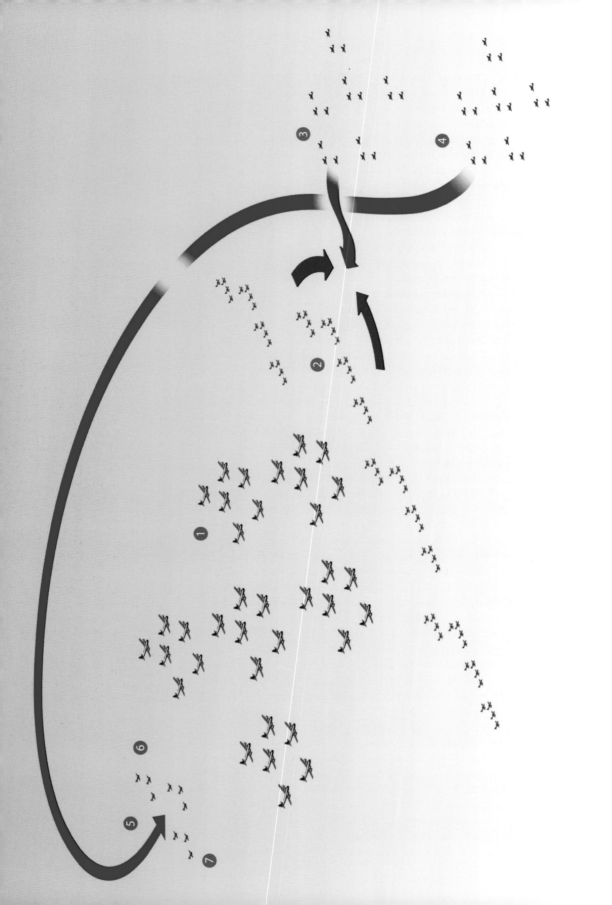

OPPOSITE FIGHTER ESCORT: THE LEMAY WAY

Once airstrips on Iwo Jima made it possible to escort B-29s during daylight missions, the US Army Air Force developed a unique and effective technique for escorting the bomber. The P-51 escort would fly sweeps ahead of the bomber formation. Japanese fighter interceptors had to fight through a swarm of US fighters to make their favored head-on attack on the American bomber formation – a task the interceptors found almost impossible. To reach the bombers the interceptors had to fly around the escorting fighters, which forced the Japanese to attack from astern. This resulted in a slow closing rate, making the Japanese easy targets for the computer-assisted defensive guns of the B-29s.

EVENTS
1. B-29 bomber formation moving at cruising speed (290mph).
2. P-51 escorts ahead of the bombers, above and level with the bombers.
3. Japanese interceptors attempting to attack from ahead had to fight through the fighters first.
4. Alternatively interceptors could fly around the fighters.
5. The bomber formation's speed forced interceptors flying around the fighters to attack from astern.
6. Fast Japanese fighters (Mitsubishi *Raiden*, or Kawanishi *Shiden*) would close at 80 to 100mph.
7. Slower fighters (Mitsubishi Zero, Nakajima *Hayabusa*, Kawasaki *Hein*) would close at 40 to 60mph.

equipment. The district was crowded with hundreds of small, home-based manufacturing machine shops. By morning, 11.4 square miles of the arsenal district was in ashes.

Two nights later the bombers were back. This time the southern end of Tokyo and the adjacent seaside manufacturing city of Kawasaki was in the cross hairs. The target contained more manufacturing, along with docks and warehouses. Three wings, with 303 B-29s, attacked. Six square miles of Tokyo and 3.6 square miles in Kawasaki were burned. Yokohama, one of Japan's largest shipbuilding centers, also lost 1.5 square miles to fire, spillover from blazes started in Kawasaki.

The strategic bombing campaign was gathering momentum. XXI Bomber Command had found ways to effectively strike Japan, both through night area bombing and medium-altitude precision bombing. It had also neutralized Japan's active defenses, both fighters and antiaircraft artillery.

Operation *Starvation*: March 27–August 14

March also saw XXI Bomber Command open a new front against Japan. On March 27 1945, it launched Operation *Starvation*, the blockade of Japan's ports and waterways using naval mines air-dropped by B-29s. It was a campaign which would contribute significantly to ultimate victory over Japan.

Admiral Chester Nimitz, commanding US Navy forces in the Pacific, was Commander in Chief, Pacific Ocean Areas (CinCPOA), in charge of Allied air, land, and sea forces in the region. When the advanced echelon of XXI Bomber Command passed through Hawaii while heading to Saipan in July 1944, Nimitz proposed using B-29s to mine waterways in the Japanese Home Islands.

At the time, Army Air Force commanders were reluctant to participate. They had no objection to occasional mining missions with B-29s. XX Bomber Command flew mining missions from India. The first, in August 1944, placed mines in the Moesi River in Sumatra,

Daytime raids on Japan were often complicated by undercast, a cloud layer between the high-flying bombers and their targets on the ground. When that happened visual bombing was impossible, and bombs had to be dropped by radar, a less accurate targeting method. (AC)

When the weather was clear, bombing accuracy could be phenomenal. This strike photograph shows the results of an attack on Sumitoma Metal Company's propeller factory. Most bombs landed within the factory complex. (AC)

part of a larger mission to neutralize the area's oil refineries. Eight B-29s dropped mines; 31 others bombed the refineries. (Thirteen bombers aborted the mission.) On January 26–27, 1945, XX Bomber Command sent 77 Superfortresses to drop mines in Singapore's and Saigon's sea approaches.

General Arnold felt that Nimitz's proposed mining campaign would serve as a distraction from the B-29's primary role as a strategic bombardment tool. Haywood Hansell, at that time commanding XXI Bomber Command, concurred. They feared a repetition of what had happened in Europe, where the strategic bombers, B-17s and B-24s, kept getting drawn away from industrial targets for use in tactical missions.

The aerial mining campaign was viewed as a similar diversion to local needs of a theater commander. Arnold believed if he agreed to use B-29s for aerial mining – a tactical mission – it would become impossible to refuse requests for tactical use of B-29s from Lord Louis Mountbatten, commanding in the China–Burma–India theater, and Douglas McArthur, Nimitz's opposite number in the Southwest Pacific Area.

In September 1944, Arnold sent Nimitz's request to the Committee of Operational Analysts (COA) for a recommendation. They endorsed the plan in October, emphasizing that blockade and strategic bombardment could combine to force Japan's surrender without an invasion. (Arnold and his advisors then believed an invasion was inevitable.) Arnold became willing to use B-29s for aerial mining, but not to do it immediately. The COA recommendation involved thousands of sorties devoted to dropping mines. During late 1944, XXI Bomber Command was lucky to launch 100 B-29s on one mission; 70 bombers was more typical. Committing to mining missions on the scale recommended would eliminate strategic bombardment.

Arnold agreed to assign one group to aerial mining – when the time was right. He sent Hansell instructions to start mining operations on April 1, 1945. Hansell protested, but complied. There matters stood for the next three months. In January 1945, Nimitz again asked XXI Bomber Command to support an aerial mining campaign. This time Nimitz requested 150 sorties per month.

Nimitz's timing proved fortunate. Curtis LeMay had just taken over command of XXI Bomber Command. LeMay viewed aerial mining through a different lens than Arnold or Hansell, seeing it as an extension of strategic bombing. Most of Japan's war production material was imported from China, Southeast Asia, and the Dutch East Indies. So was much of its food. Honshu (Japan's most industrialized island) and Shikoku lacked iron ore and good-quality coal, which came from Kyushu and Hokkaido. All of it was moved by sea. Without raw materials Japan's industry would come to a halt.

Only B-29s could place mines where they were needed. The Inland Sea, the Sea of Japan, and the Korean Peninsula were out of range of other Allied aircraft. Allied submarines could penetrate these areas only at great peril. Eighty percent of Japan's merchant fleet used the strait between Kyushu and Honshu, the Shimonoseki Strait. LeMay grasped the opportunity that closing it offered.

He submitted a plan to support Nimitz. LeMay decided to devote an entire wing to drop mines. Dropping mines successfully was specialist work, requiring skilled navigation and precision bombing. LeMay chose one wing, the 313th, for all mining missions. It arrived in Tinian in late January and started its training cycle. It was equipped with AN-APQ-13 radar sets, the most advanced and accurate ground-scanning radar then operational.

The wing's four groups went through extensive training. This included time on eight simulators in Tinian and several practice missions, including one dropping an actual mine. The Navy established a depot to store the mines and assigned two officers and 40 men to assist the Air Force.

Mines were dropped using radar. A bomber found a landmark (such as an easily identified headland or mountain), flew an assigned direction over the landmark and dropped the mines at a selected drop interval based on aircraft ground speed. Each Superfortress was assigned different objectives, set prior to the mission by the wing radar navigator. They were given a translucent flimsy with the target information on it, to be placed on the radar scope. As mines were dropped, the presumed location was marked on the flimsy. These were collected and analyzed post-mission.

Three types of mines were used: 2,000lb Mark 25s and 1,000lb Mark 26s and Mark 36s. Provided by the US Navy, they were remotely triggered, using a combination of acoustic and magnetic triggers, with different sensitivity settings. The mines were set with delays between one and 30 days. Once armed, a ship counter was activated, randomly set at one to nine ships. If the count was five, the first four vessels passed over the mines unharmed, the mine detonating when the fifth ship passed. The mines lacked sterilizers (to detonate the mine after a preset time). They were dangerous until they were swept or found a target.

The first mine mission was flown on March 27. It was a night mission, as were all mining operations. The target was the Shimonoseki Strait. Of the 105 B-29s sent, 97 dropped mines. The bombers dropped mines at altitudes between 4,900 and 8,000ft. While flak was moderate to heavy over some landmarks, it fell away once the bombers were over the water. Three B-29s were seriously damaged, five lightly damaged, and three shot down by antiaircraft fire. Fighter interference was negligible. Seventy-three fighters were sighted but

Operation *Starvation* mining mission

Naval mining, embraced by Curtis LeMay, was a major deviation from Army Air Force doctrine, but it proved devastatingly effective.

LeMay assigned an entire wing to dropping the mines, having them specialize in the practice. They were equipped with the high-accuracy AN-APQ-13 radar navigation and bombing equipment, and trained on precision dropping of mines using radar.

The bombers carried 1,000lb MK 26 and MK 36 mines and 2,000lb MK 25 mines, with up to 12 1,000lb mines, seven 2,000lb mines or a mix of the two sizes up to 14,000lb. They were dropped at night from medium altitude. The bombers were occasionally molested by fighters or flak, but this was rare.

This plate shows a B-29 dropping its mines in the Shimonoseki Strait during the first mining mission on March 27, 1945. This bomber is one of 31 belonging to the 9th Bomber Group, 313th Wing which flew this mission as part of Force Charlie. In all a total of 55 B-29s from the 313th Bombardment Wing flew this first mission. They dropped a total of 549 MK 26 and MK 36 mines and 276 MK 25 mines.

The aircraft is making its run over the strait. Drops had to be precisely targeted, as navigation error left gaps in the minefield. Mines were dropped at altitudes between 4,900ft and 8,000ft. The B-29 flew a straight line along a precalculated heading from a known landmark, releasing mines at times predetermined by mission planners at Guam. Drop times were recorded for post-mission analysis. Mine runs lasted from one to 16 minutes.

If you look carefully, a *Hein* fighter is in the background. There was a *Hein* unit at Ashia Airfield on Honshu just north of the Shimonoseki Strait. It was scrambled in response to the raid. The *Hein*, a single-engine daytime fighter with a crew of one (the pilot) had no radar. During this mission *Heins* were spotted by crews of mine-carrying bombers. Of 73 fighters seen by bomber crews only 13 attacked, and those all missed. The other 60 flew past without attacking, like this one. Japanese pilots either missed seeing the B-29s or declined to attack them.

Admiral Chester Nimitz (speaking to General Henry "Hap" Arnold [left] on Guam) was an early advocate of using B-29s to close Japan's waterways through aerially dropped mines. Nimitz first raised the issue in July 1944. By April 1945, Operation *Starvation* was under way and already successful. (USNHHC)

only 13 attacked, and no B-29s were damaged by Japanese fighters. One *Hein* was reported shot down.

Two minefields were laid, Minefield Mike on the western entrance to the strait and Minefield Love on the eastern side. A total of 825 mines were dropped in the straits. Roughly two-thirds were 1,000lb mines. Additionally, 50 mines were jettisoned in designated drop areas to prevent friendly casualties. Mike was laid as planned, but Love had a 3-mile gap, due to a drop failure by one B-29. The gap was filled two days later on the second mine mission.

That mission saw 85 B-29s mine the Inland Sea, the body of water between Honshu, Shikoku, and Kyshu. In addition to closing the gap in Minefield Love, mines were dropped off the sea approaches to Hiroshima, Sasebo, and Kure. Hiroshima was a merchant and naval port; Sasebo and Kure two of the Imperial Japanese Navy's most important bases.

Phase I of Operation *Starvation* ran until May 7. During Phase I, the 313th Wing flew 246 sorties in seven missions, dropping a total of 2,039 mines. Mines completely blocked the Shimonoseki Strait and important ports on the eastern part of the Inland Sea. Only eight ships were sunk in the Shimonoseki Strait during the first two weeks after Operation *Starvation* opened, because the Japanese shut down the strait for two weeks to sweep it after realizing it was mined.

Traffic through the strait dropped by 90 percent after that. The 313th reseeded the strait with more mines, a process which continued until the war ended. Seventy percent of Japan's shipping was being rerouted to ports outside the Inland Sea on the coast of the Sea of Japan. The goods ships carried had to be moved by rail to Inland Sea ports where the factories expecting them were located, further overloading Japan's rail network.

Shutting the Shimonoseki Strait also affected Imperial Japanese Navy operations. When the battleship *Yamato* left Kure on its April 7 sortie against the US beachhead on Okinawa

A 2,000lb Mark 25 mine displayed at the National Museum of the Air Force in Dayton, Ohio. This was one of the critical components in closing Japan's straits and harbors. (NMUSAF)

it was forced to exit the Inland Sea through the eastern Bungo Strait. It was spotted by a B-29 returning from a mission, whose crew reported the sighting. US Army–Navy rivalries, unlike those of Japan, did not prevent the Army Air Force from quickly passing the word to the Navy, who found and sank the super-battleship with carrier aircraft.

Phase I of Operation *Starvation* was the beginning. Phase II began on May 7 and continued for nine days. New minefields were sown interdicting Kobe, Osaka, Nagoya, and Tokyo Bay. Nine of Japan's ten largest industrial cities were blockaded by mines. Only Fukuoka, on Kyushu's west coast, remained open to ships. These new mines were fused with a new pressure fuse believed "unsweepable," impossible to remove through conventional minesweeping.

Phase III started on May 13 and ran until June 6. Seven missions were flown, closing Honshu's Sea of Japan ports. Minefields were sown in Maizuru, Miyazu, Tsuruga, Niiagata, Nanao, Fushiki, and Karatsu

A B-29 drops a 1,000lb Mark 26 mine during Operation *Starvation*. Shutting the Shimonoseki Strait crippled Japan's ability to move vital cargoes. (USAAF)

harbors on Honshu, and Fukuoka and Moji harbors, and the He-Saki anchorage on Kyushu. Rerouting ships became more difficult, as there were few safe ports to which vessels could be sent.

Instead of wing-strength missions involving all four groups of the wing, these minefields were sown by single groups. Plans to mine Tokyo Harbor and the Pacific ports were dropped. There was too little sea traffic to justify using mines better placed elsewhere.

Phase IV, which ran from June 7 through July 8, intensified the Kyushu–Honshu west coast blockades. Minefields were added at Kamatsu, Senzaki, Yuya Bay, Sakai, Obama, Hagi, and Sakata. Existing minefields on the Sea of Japan were thickened, and minefields in the Shimonoseki Strait and Inland Sea were reinforced. Thirteen group-sized missions of 20 to 30 aircraft were flown.

Phase V ran to the end of the war, completing the blockade, closing the final ports on Honshu, and mining ports on the northeast coast of Korea. To allow more remote locations to be reached, the bombers, which took off from Tinian, landed at Iwo Jima to refuel before heading home.

The Japanese could not easily counter these barriers. The only way the pressure-fused mines could be swept was by detonating them with a ship – a grim illustration of the adage "every ship is a minesweeper, once." When they thought they had a channel cleared, a previously inert mine on a long-time delay activated, and damaged or sank a ship in a channel thought swept.

Over the campaign 12,135 mines were laid: nearly 5,400 in the Shimonoseki Strait, 2,300 in the Inland Sea, and almost 4,000 around ports on the Sea of Japan. A total of 1,529 sorties were flown, with only 15 bombers lost to all causes. Twenty-six minefields were laid. The mines sank or permanently disabled 670 ships carrying an aggregate of over 1.25 million tons of cargo space. More importantly, by the end of the campaign virtually no sea traffic was leaving or arriving in Japan. In February, Japanese monthly shipping tonnage was 520,000 tons; by August it was only 8,000 tons.

Look Homeward Angel, 6th Bomb Group, 313th Wing after an emergency landing at Okinawa. LeMay gave the job of dropping mines to the 313th Bombardment Wing. While it flew standard missions, including incendiary raids and precision bombardment, it specialized in mine-laying. (NARA)

Airfield interruption: April 16–May 11

Just as the strategic bombing campaign was gathering momentum, XXI Bomber Command had to pause it. For three weeks, from April 16 to May 9, the B-29s went after a new target, Japanese airfields in Kyushu, to assist the Allied forces invading Okinawa.

US Marine Corps troops and US Army soldiers landed on Okinawa in the Ryukyu Islands on April 1, 1945. The invasion started smoothly, but quickly got bogged down due to stiff Japanese resistance. The island, part of a chain separating the East China Sea from the Philippine Sea, was considered part of Japan proper. It was part of the Okinawa Prefecture; the equivalent of a state in the United States. Okinawa elected representatives to Japan's Imperial Diet, Japan's legislative assembly.

From Okinawa, aircraft – other than B-29s – could reach Kyushu, but this also meant aircraft from Kyushu could reach Okinawa. Aircraft at bases on Shikoku could stage to Kyushu, refuel and reach Okinawa. Waves of Japanese aircraft from Kyushu and Shikoku were regularly attacking the Allied fleet off Okinawa.

By August, Japan's merchant fleet was either sunk, damaged and unable to go to sea, or hiding in port. *Shinyu Maru*, a war-emergency construction, is shown in Hiroshima Harbor, one of many ships trapped in port by mines laid by B-29s. (USNHHC)

Japanese pilots lacked the skill to bomb ships accurately. Japan solved that problem with the kamikaze corps. Instead of bombing them, pilots crashed into ships, converting a bomb-laden aircraft into a cruise missile with a human pilot replacing a digital computer for guidance. Kamikaze tactics permitted obsolescent aircraft (since they were not coming back anyway) and those with a round-trip range too short to reach Okinawa and return (it was a one-way trip) to be used. It was a relatively efficient use of barely trained pilots, as massive Allied air superiority meant rookie Japanese pilots rarely survived their first combat mission, even when flying conventional aircraft.

Nimitz wanted kamikazes stopped before take-off by suppressing the airfields they flew from. The newly captured Okinawa airfields lacked the infrastructure (or supplies) for combat missions against Kyushu. Aircraft carrier strikes against Kyushu and Shikoku airfields were risky and limited. A maximum effort by the Pacific fleet with 11 fleet carriers and six light carriers could deliver only 300 tons of bombs daily on the airfields. By mid-April, a maximum effort strike by XXI Bomber Command could deliver 3,000 tons.

The Army Air Force resisted tactical use of B-29s. XXI Bomber Command launched two raids against Iwo Jima in the run-up to invading the Bonin Islands, but only one bombed the island's fortifications, the other hitting airfields. These raids were primarily to prevent Iwo Jima from being used to stage Japanese bombing raids against B-29 bases. The fortifications raid involved 20 Superfortresses, and the airfield raid 30.

When LeMay was asked to support both the Iwo Jima and Okinawa invasions, he enthusiastically agreed. He supported both invasions by bombing Japanese aircraft factories, arguing that reducing available aircraft would weaken Japanese resistance. This allowed the Army Air Force to continue strategic bombardment under the guise of tactical support.

It worked to keep the Superfortresses attacking targets in Japan. Now, with Navy losses mounting due to kamikazes, Nimitz wanted relief, which he believed only B-29s could provide. Nimitz complained to Admiral Ernest King, Commander-in-Chief of the United States Navy. King complained to the other Joint Chiefs of Staff, who directed Arnold to cooperate with Nimitz. Arnold told LeMay to bomb the airfields.

From April 16 until May 11, XXI Bomber Command attacked Japanese airfields on Kyushu and Shikoku. The attacks did not affect Operation *Starvation*: Nimitz wanted mining given a priority. Since mining missions fitted LeMay's conception of strategic bombardment, LeMay was glad to continue them with the 313th Wing. The other XXI Bomber Command wings, the 73rd and 314th, were stuck attacking the airfields.

LeMay objected to bombing airfields because high-altitude airfield bombardment did limited damage. A wing of B-29s could drop lots of explosives on a target, but were not that accurate. Bombing visually, most of the bombs dropped would land within the perimeter of the airfield, but hits on individual buildings were not guaranteed. With radar bombing, the only guarantee that could be made was that some bombs would land on the runways.

At Rabaul in early 1944, Allied bombers devastated aircraft on the ground at Japanese airfields. Success depended upon surprise achieved due to the tree-top altitudes at which the bombers – twin-engine B-25s and Beaufighters – flew and the then-primitive Japanese early-warning radar. B-29s were not designed for wave-top or tree-top operations, and Japanese radar was much more sophisticated by 1945.

Japanese signal intelligence gave a minimum four hours' warning of an inbound raid through monitoring B-29 radio activity. It gave time to service and fuel all aircraft on an airfield capable of flying. Early-warning radar alerted defenders that B-29s were within 30 minutes of the Kyushu coast. The half-hour radar warning provided time to launch all aircraft

The greatest hazard to the men flying the Superfortress was the long, over-ocean flight. Minor battle damage or mechanical failure often resulted in a water landing short of the home runway. A lucky crew from a ditched B-29 awaits rescue after being found by a patrolling flying boat. (AC)

On March 4, 1945 *Dinah Might*, shown here, became the first Superfortress to land on Iwo Jima. There were 2,400 B-29 emergency landings at Iwo Jima airstrips, involving nearly 25,000 airmen. (NARA)

before the B-29s arrived at an airfield. Kamikaze aircraft and their escorts flew east and north, away from the oncoming bombers and their escorting fighters, preserved to fight another day.

The B-29s would arrive over the empty airfield, drop their bombs, and head home. They attacked at high altitude because LeMay did not wish to risk his bombers to flak. In April and May there was almost always cloud cover over the airfields, so attacks were always radar-aimed. The runways would be cratered, but the Japanese filled in the craters and the airfield was active the next day.

LeMay gave it a real try. Between the start of the airfield campaign and May 19, when Nimitz finally released the B-29s, XXI Bomber Command flew 16 raids on Japanese airfields. The first two on April 17 and April 18 were one-wing efforts with over 100 bombers. Two others, on April 21 and April 26, were all-hands efforts against airfields with 215 and 195 bombers respectively. Six others were one-wing efforts; of these, four saw at least 100 bombers attack. By May, one-group missions were being flown, probably because there was so little perceived to be left to hit.

The value of the airfield raids was psychological rather than substantial. Japanese kamikaze attacks trailed off as the campaign continued. The Japanese were running out of aircraft and wanted to husband the ones they did have to protect Kyushu against the expected invasion. It left Nimitz happy because he believed it had taken heat off the fleet guarding Okinawa. It also left the Japanese happy because the US was wasting bombs on already cratered runways rather than Japanese cities and factories. The bomber crews were happy because these missions were "milk runs," and they needed the break.

Besides the airfield and mining missions, XXI Bomber Command flew five strategic bombardment missions during this period: an April 24 attack against the Tachikawa Aircraft Factory at Tachikawa, Japan, in which 101 aircraft dropped bombs; a May 5 mission, when 148 aircraft bombed the Hiro Naval Aircraft Factory; and three May 10 missions against Tokuyama, Otaki, and Amami.

The April 24 raid took place because Kyushu was clouded over. Clear skies were predicted over Toyko near the Tachikawa factory, which built radial engines for Army aircraft. The B-29s bombed from 12,000ft, the low altitude allowing the formation to bomb visually in hazy skies. Flak and fighters downed four Superfortresses and damaged 68 others, but the cost was worth it. The factory, which averaged 250 engines per month, was destroyed and production ceased.

The May 5 attack on the Hiro Naval Aircraft Factory was coordinated with airfield strikes on Kyushu. The bombers came in at 20,000ft and dropped 578 tons of 1,000lb and 2,000lb general-purpose bombs. The factory was badly damaged and production was cut in half; over 500 assembly machines were destroyed.

In April two new wings arrived in the Marianas. The 58th Bombardment Wing had been sent to India and China in 1944. When XX Bomber Command deactivated, the wing transferred to Tinian. The ground element arrived in early April, and aircraft and flight crews later that month. It flew its first mission from Tinian on May 5, 1945, when 53 aircraft from two of its groups joined 117 B-29s from the 73rd Bomb Wing in bombing the Hiro Naval Aircraft factory in Kure.

The 315th Bombardment Wing also began arriving in April, when its air service groups arrived at Guam. Ground echelons and air elements would not arrive until May. It flew its first Japan-bound mission in June.

The ground elements of the 509th Composite Group also arrived in April. The rest of the unit drifted in during June and July. Its aircraft were modified to drop the atomic bomb. It flew practice missions in June and July, including combat strikes over Japan, single-aircraft missions dropping one large bomb, simulating dropping an atomic bomb. It ultimately flew two atomic missions, both in August.

The airfield attacks had several positive benefits for XXI Bomber Command. It allowed ordnance stores to be replenished, especially incendiaries. The success of the urban attacks caused the production of incendiaries and the quantities delivered to be increased significantly. By the end of April, the flow of incendiaries and other bombs had opened to a flood. Ordnance delivery was streamlined, with bombs going directly from ammunition ships to the airfields.

More critical was aircrew availability. In March a maximum strike used 300 aircraft; in May it exceeded 450. April saw 152 new crews arrive – enough to man the new bombers – but in May an additional 282 crews were needed, while only 106 were expected to arrive. Aircrew, rather than ordnance and aircraft, threatened to be the offensive's limiting factor.

LeMay responded by increasing aircrew monthly flight hours. Maximum recommended flying hours for aircrew was 60 hours per month, but in March, aircrew flew 80 hours.

Missions ended with bomber crews briefing intelligence officers about what they saw and did during each mission. Individual crews were debriefed around a trestle table at their base's operations shed. (AC)

Crowded construction and flammable material in the houses of Japan's poor made major Japanese cities vulnerable to incendiary attack. In the most densely packed cities of the United States during the 1940s no more than 15 percent of a typical square mile was roofed over. In Japanese cities it sometimes reached 80 percent. (AC)

LeMay decided to maintain that flight rate, keeping crews in the air 80 hours or more each month. This change increased capacity by a third. Flight surgeons warned that six consecutive months at that rate could burn out the crews. However, LeMay was betting that if higher flight rates were maintained only six months of missions would be needed: the war would be over by then.

The Japanese used the respite granted their aircraft factories by the airfield raids to increase Home Defense fighter strength. They replaced losses and increased fighters assigned to interception units by 130 to a total of 480 by May. Most replacements were new types such as the *Hayate* and *Shiden*. Yet Japan did not reform its air defense system. Army and Navy aircraft were still not pooled, and fighters were expected to find bombers with minimal guidance from the ground and were still assigned geographically. Geographic assignment did frustrate US efforts to lure fighters away from targets by diversionary raids. But it ensured bomber formations were attacked by numbers too small to saturate US defenses even when met by the full fighter strength of a Japanese defensive area.

Fire bombing resumed: May 11–June 7

Nimitz released the B-29s from airfield attacks on May 11. Three days later, LeMay started a month-long bombing campaign focused on Japan's ten largest cities. Over the next 30 days, 11 major missions were flown. Seven missions saw more than 400 bombers attack, and none involved fewer than 100 aircraft. Having found ways to successfully bomb Japan, LeMay conducted an unrelenting campaign against Japan's industrial cities. When clear weather was predicted, daylight precision missions were flown. When clouds were forecast, an area incendiary raid took place.

LeMay had four wings: the 58th, 73rd, 313th, and 314th, each of which could send 100 or more aircraft on one mission. The newly arrived 58th Bomb Wing was sending 140 or more aircraft out per mission by mid-May. With incendiary stocks refilled, XXI Bomber Command could conduct bigger fire raids.

LeMay anticipated the end of airfield raids by a day, on May 10 sending out three wings on three different missions in different locations. The 58th Wing conducted a raid against the oil storage facilities at Oshima on the northern Ryukyu chain. Meanwhile, the 73rd Wing attacked the Third Naval Depot at Tokuyama, while the 314th Wing bombed the Army Fuel Depot at Iwakuni. All three were daylight precision attacks, using a mix of general-purpose and incendiary bombs to destroy petroleum storage facilities. The worst performance destroyed 20 percent of the fuel and tanks at Tokyama. The best performance was turned in by the 58th Bomb Wing, which destroyed 90 percent of the fuel and tanks at Oshima.

The first target in the new incendiary campaign was Nagoya on May 14. All four wings sent aircraft. A total of 529 B-29s took off, with 472 dropping bombs on the target: 2,511 tons of M-69 incendiaries with clusters set to open at 1,000ft.

It was a daylight attack to obtain better bombing accuracy and confuse Japanese air defense. The raid was intended to destroy the industrial area in northern Nagoya around Nagoya Castle. Primary objectives included the Mitsubishi Aircraft Engine Works, the Mitsubishi Electrical Company, and the Chigusa branch of the Nagoya Arsenal. Because it was a daylight attack, bombing density was high. All 472 aircraft dropped their bombs during an 80-minute window. (Two previous night incendiary raids, with just under 300 bombers, each lasted almost three hours from first to last bomb.) Smoke from fires that early bombers started led later ones to bomb using radar.

Results were not as good as hoped, largely due to the efficient response by the Nagoya Fire Department. Just over three square miles were burned out. The raid seriously damaged the Mitsubishi Aircraft Engine Works. Intelligence identified 131 separate blazes started: one became uncontrollable, but was eventually stopped at a firebreak.

Mission losses were relatively heavy. The aircraft came in at between 12,000 and 20,500ft, altitudes where Japanese fighters were effective. One B-29 was shot down by a fighter and another was downed by flak. Eight others were lost to other causes, including aircraft forced to ditch as a result of damage received. In all, 68 returning aircraft were damaged. Yet given Nagoya's damage, it was an acceptable exchange rate.

Nagoya was revisited for a fifth and final fire raid two days later. On the evening of May 16, 522 B-29s took off from Marianas bases, with 457 attacking Nagoya, the primary target. This time the objective was the docks and industrial regions in the city's southeast quadrant. The area contained many significant targets: the Mitsubishi Aircraft Works, the Atsuta factory of the Aichi Aircraft Company, the Nippon Vehicle Company, and the Atsuta branch of the Nagoya Arsenal.

The aircraft attacked at lower altitudes for greater accuracy. The low elements were assigned an altitude of 6,600ft, while the highest wing came in at 18,300ft. Many of the late-arriving low element aircraft were forced higher by thermal drafts and dense smoke. The primary bomb load was M-76 incendiaries, 500lb bombs filled with white phosphorus and asphalt.

Nagoya was the city best-prepared for incendiary attacks. Wide fire lanes kept clear of burnable material and canals too wide for flames to cross contained fires. When a fire jumped a barrier, firefighters could often keep it from spreading beyond the initial breach. (AC)

Tokyo Bay

Edogawa River

Kyuedo River

Shinnaka River

Naka River

Arakawa River

Sumida River

Tama River

EDOGAWA

KATSUSHIKA

MUKOJIMA

JOTO

ADACHI

ASAKUSA

HONJO

FUKAGAWA

ARAKAWA

SHITAYA

NIHONBASHI

OJI

HONGO

KANDA

KYOBASHI

TAKINGAWA

KOISHIKAWA

USHIGOME

KOJIMACHI
(AND IMPERIAL
PALACE)

SHINAGAWA

YOTSUYA

AKASAKA

AZABU

SHIBA

TOSHIMA

NAKANO

YODOBASHI

SHIBUYA

MEGUR

EBARA

OMORI

KAMATA

ITABASHI

SUGINAMI

SETAGAYA

N

2 miles

2km

0

City limits

Burned-out areas prior to March 10, 1945 raid

Burned-out areas due to March 10, 1945 raid

Burned-out areas due to April 14 and April 15, 1945 raids

Burned-out areas due to May 24 and May 26, 1945 raids

OPPOSITE TOKYO BURNED

Planners believed these heavy bombs would crack through heavily built factory buildings to set fires inside. Of the 3,534 tons of incendiaries dropped, 3,407 tons were M-76s.

Results were impressive. Nearly 4 square miles of Nagoya's harbor area was burned out from the 138 major fires started by the incendiaries. Mitsubishi's aircraft works was heavily damaged. In four earlier fire raids 12 square miles of Nagoya were incinerated; now the total was 16 square miles. The city was lucky because winds triggering major fire storms were absent during all five fire raids. B-29s returned to Nagoya six more times, but these were precision strikes. There was not enough contiguous unburnt built-up urban area left in Nagoya to make a sixth incendiary raid worthwhile.

On May 19, the B-29s took a break from incendiary raids, launching a precision raid on the Tachikawa Aircraft Company in Hamamatsu. Two hundred and seventy-two B-29s were sent, escorted by 100 P-51s. Weather forced the escort to return to Iwo Jima and obscured the factory. Bombs were dropped by radar on Hamamatsu's urban area.

The incendiary campaign returned to Tokyo on May 23. In the biggest raid yet, 562 B-29s left the Marianas, 520 reaching Tokyo. The raid involved all four groups of all four wings. The target was Tokyo's dock and industrial district south of the Imperial Palace compound on the west side of Tokyo Bay. This mission repeated the M-47 and M-69 mix used in previous Tokyo fire raids. Forty-four pathfinders dropped M-47s to mark the target. The rest of the bomber force was primarily armed with M-69s. Incendiary clusters were fused to open at 5,000ft.

The bombers came in low: between 7,800 and 15,100ft. The weather was bad and the target was almost completely overcast, so all bombing was done by radar. Flak was intense, but the Japanese were firing blind. Many night fighters were also present. Over 3,600 tons of incendiaries landed on Tokyo's southern sector, comprising over 2,800 tons of M-69s and nearly 800 tons of M47 bombs. The bombers dropped their payload for nearly two hours. By sunrise on May 24, just over 5 square miles of Tokyo's docks and factories were burned out.

The B-29s returned the night of May 25–26. This time 502 bombers took off and 464 reached Tokyo, the first arriving shortly after midnight. The attack began with M-47s to start major fires. In addition to 1,320 tons of M-69s, 945 tons of M-50s and 350 tons of M-76 incendiaries were added to the mix. The M-50 was a 4lb thermite incendiary, dropped in clusters like the M-69. It was the first time the bomb was used against Tokyo. Clusters were fused at 5,000ft.

The target area was north and west of the previous mission's target, containing a mix of governmental, financial, and commercial buildings, as well as homes and factories. The weather was better:

The final fire mission against Tokyo occurred after midnight on May 27, 1945. This photograph shows Tokyo's southern districts fully engulfed in flame on that night. (LOC)

cloud cover was lighter, only 30 percent. The aircraft came in higher, between 8,000 and 22,000ft. It was the most successful raid yet, more than 16 square miles of urban Tokyo being destroyed by flames. As with the previous mission, Japanese opposition was fierce. Since the skies were clearer, Japanese antiaircraft fire was more accurate, the heaviest yet reported on a B-29 mission.

Losses on both missions were heavy. Seventeen B-29s failed to return on May 24; 69 were damaged. On May 26, 26 B-29s were lost and 100 damaged. It was a marked contrast to the light losses at Nagoya. The nearly three-hour length of the Tokyo missions, combined with the massive numbers of bombers over Tokyo, made a perfect environment for Japanese night fighters. The low altitude also favored them: they were bound to find something. The 3 percent bomber loss rate on May 24–25 and 5.5 percent losses on May 26–27 were tolerable, offset by over 22 square miles of Tokyo destroyed.

As with Nagoya, Tokyo was then removed from the area bombing target list. There were too few urban spaces with enough contiguous unburnt area to make another area raid worthwhile. LeMay instead unleashed his bombers on a new target: Yokohama.

Yokohama, Japan's fifth-largest city and second-largest port, was a major shipbuilding, automotive, petroleum-refining, and chemical industry center. Concerned about the high losses of the Tokyo raid, LeMay planned a high-altitude daytime strike. XXI Bomber Command struck Yokohama on May 29, sending 517 bombers in group formations, spaced four minutes apart, carrying a mix of M-47 and M-69 incendiaries. They were escorted by 101 P-51s from Iwo Jima.

A major naval base, Yokohama was defended by the Navy. An estimated 150 Zeroes attempted to stop the bombers. A fighter melee ensued with the Mustangs losing three, while claiming 26 kills. (The numbers of Zeroes attacking and shot down were probably exaggerated.) The Japanese fighters also shot down five B-29s and damaged 175 others.

The 454 B-29s dropped 2,570 tons of incendiaries on Yokohama's waterfront and business district, burning out almost 7 square miles of Yokohama's 20 square miles of urban area. The weather was unusually clear, allowing the first groups to bomb visually. Smoke from fires started forced later groups to use radar bombing.

Osaka was the target two days later. To precisely focus on remaining unburnt districts, this was another daytime raid. Each wing was assigned different targets. The objective was the industrial areas along the Yodo River, filled with warehouses, docks, petroleum plants, and shipyards. Different mixes of incendiaries were carried, depending on buildings in the wing's target area, but all bombers carried a few fragmentation clusters, ordered to be dropped first and intended to discourage firefighting.

This mission was to be escorted, but the 148 P-51s accompanying them ran into a storm front and flew into an undetected thunderstorm. Twenty-seven P-51s crashed, 94 were forced to return to Iwo Jima, and only 27 Mustangs reached Osaka to protect the bombers. Ten bombers were lost to enemy action.

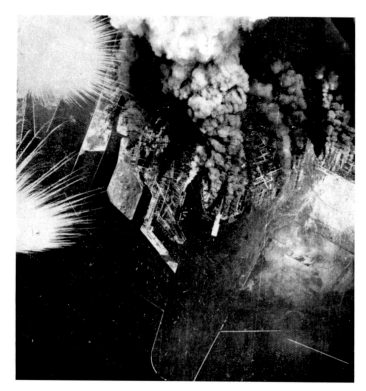

Osaka was struck by 458 B-29s on June 1, 1945. This daytime fire raid focused on burning out industrial areas along the Yodo River. This photograph, taken during the raid, shows a mission successful in burning out Osaka's waterfront. (AC)

The view from the cockpit of a B-29 during the June 5 Kobe raid. Another daytime mission, the B-29s bombed in formation. Towering clouds of smoke indicate the success of this incendiary mission. (AC)

Of 509 B-29s launched, 458 bombed Osaka, delivering 3,157 tons of munitions. Bombing altitudes ranged from 18,000 to 28,000ft. Osaka had over 3 square miles burned, with spillover into the neighboring city of Amagasaki. Over 4,200 factories were destroyed, most of which were small, but several were large facilities.

Night raid over Akashi

Shortly after midnight on July 7, 1945, four groups of the 73rd Wing, 124 B-29s, including 12 pathfinder planes, began an incendiary raid on the Kyushu town of Akashi. In 1945 Akashi had a population of 84,000, which included 40,000 workers at the Kawasaki aircraft factory in the town. Between 12.15am and 1.27am the raiders dropped 975.9 tons of M-69 incendiaries from altitudes ranging from 6,900 to 8,200ft. The B-29s approached in a bomber stream of individual aircraft, with the pathfinders first. The rest of the aircraft passed over the target city in roughly 30-second intervals, aiming at areas near but outside the fires already burning.

The raid devastated Akashi. By sunrise, nearly 60 percent of the city was in ashes. This included the city's residential core. Over 9,000 houses, ten factories and four waterfront warehouses were destroyed. As it was, Akashi got lucky. A light rain helped contain the fires, and a steady, light north by northwest wind allowed firefighters to predict the direction of the fires and get ahead of them. The raid caused relatively few casualties. By July 7, the Twentieth Air Force was dropping leaflets warning a town would be attacked the following day. Once radar warned the Japanese that aircraft were heading towards Akashi an orderly evacuation occurred, with a third of the city's residents sheltering in a park north of the city or at the waterfront to the south.

The aircraft in this plate is *Thumper*, Tail code A21, Serial number 42-24623. It belonged to the 870th Squadron of the 497th Bombardment Group in the 73rd Very Heavy Bombardment Wing, Twentieth Air Force. The aircraft featured artwork of the rabbit Thumper from the Walt Disney cartoon, *Bambi*. *Thumper* would survive the war having completed 44 missions, including participating in fire raids on Tokyo and Nagoya. It is shown dropping its clusters of M-69 incendiaries.

Arriving during the middle of the raid, it would have flown over the city when it was fully ablaze. Light from the flames illuminated the bomber's belly and the undersides of its wings. By this stage of the war, active enemy resistance had virtually disappeared. The mission was unopposed.

Kobe was next, attacked on June 5. This time 530 B-29s took off, 473 bombing the target. The unescorted daytime mission went in lower than average for a daytime strike. The bombers dropped at altitudes between 13,500 and 18,000ft. They dropped 3,077 tons of incendiaries, burning out just over 4 square miles. With previous damage, over half the city was in ashes. Kobe was thereafter removed from the fire-bombing target list. The unescorted B-29s ran into heavy Japanese fighter opposition, nine bombers being shot down and two lost to operational accidents.

Osaka was revisited on June 7, with 449 bombers sent. This time three wings carried incendiaries, while one wing was loaded with explosives. The latter wing's target was the Osaka Army Arsenal in the eastern section of the town, which was surrounded by transportation targets, munitions works, and other industrial targets. The bombers were escorted by 138 P-51s, but the Mustangs proved unnecessary, as heavy low clouds kept the Japanese fighters on the ground. Eleven B-29s were damaged by flak, but none were shot down. Undercast forced the 409 bombers that attacked to use radar targeting. This proved very effective, the 2,540 tons dropped burning out over 2 square miles and destroying over 1,000 industrial buildings.

Knockout: June 8–August 14

The maximum-effort area bombing campaign against Japan's large cities ended with the Osaka June 7 raid. Six of Japan's ten largest cities had been burned out, these six cities having no remaining contiguous unburned territory meriting a maximum-effort raid. Two other top-ten cities, Kyoto and Hiroshima, were spared, Kyoto because of its cultural significance and Hiroshima was being preserved as an atomic bomb target.

A bomb bay view of the June 5 Kobe raid. Incendiaries rain down on Kobe's harbor. (AC)

The remaining two, Fukuoka and Yawata, were among the smallest cities in the top ten (eighth and tenth largest respectively), and on Kyushu's west coast. Their turn would come, but both were too small to merit a maximum-effort raid. Two wings were enough for either target.

Even as raids reduced the big cities to rubble, XXI Bomber Command planners were preparing the next phase of the strategic bombing campaign. Meteorologists predicted the summer monsoon would keep Japan covered with clouds on most days from June to August. Planners built two lists of targets: industrial and military targets to be hit by daytime strikes and secondary cities with enough industry to make a nighttime area attack worthwhile. This allowed maximum flexibility in mission planning. Since no target merited a four-wing maximum-effort strike, the planners scheduled multiple missions on a single day.

The first two days implementing this "Empire Plan" involved daylight raids, B-29s striking nine different aircraft factories.

On June 9, 110 B-29s conducted attacks against three aircraft factories in different cities: Narao, Atsuta, and Akashi. Two groups destroyed the Kawanishi Aircraft Company's plant at Narao and two other groups flattened Aichi's Atsuta factory in Nagoya. The single group sent to Akashi to bomb the Kawasaki plant there found the target clouded over. They bombed using radar, hitting the town instead of the factory.

The next day 280 B-29s, escorted by 107 P-51s, were sent to bomb six different targets in the Tokyo Bay area. The 73rd wing bombed the Nakajima's Musashino factory. Single bomb groups were sent after five other aircraft factories: Tokyo's Tachikawa Army Air Arsenal, two more Nakajima plants (at Ogikubu and Omiya), Japan Aircraft Company's Tomioka factory, and the Hitachi Aircraft plant at Chiba. The three Nakajima plants were covered

By June 1945, Japan's civilians were aware the war was going badly. While workers still stood outside the offices of the Tokyo Minichi and read posted newspaper accounts of glorious victories by the Imperial armed forces, their own experiences told a different story. (AC)

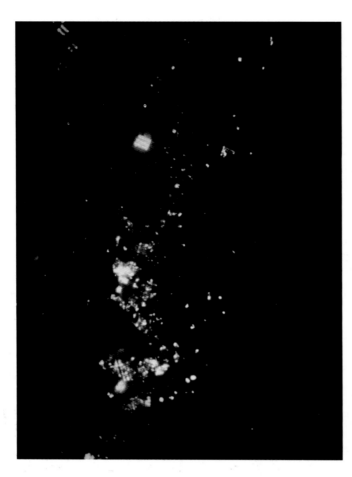

Ube, an industrial town of 100,000 inhabitants in 1945, was hit on July 1. This picture shows the fires started early in the attack. Nearly a quarter of the city burned. (AC)

by clouds, so those Superfortresses switched to radar targets: a seaplane base at Kasumigaura and Hitachi's Kaigan engineering works. Heavy damage was done to all targets, whether bombed visually or by radar.

Five days later, a final firebombing raid was conducted against Osaka. So little was left of the city that it was not the sole target. One set of bombers went after Osaka, while other units bombed Amagasaki. This marked the first multi-city incendiary raids, albeit with two cities close to each other. Over 3,150 tons of incendiaries were dropped on the two cities by 444 bombers. Osaka had another almost 2 square miles of urban area burned out, while Amagasaki lost more than half a square mile. Osaka was removed from the area bombing target list.

This was followed by two massive sets of incendiary raids over the nights of June 17–18 and 18–19 with seven cities hit; four the first night, three the second.

Marianas airfields launched 477 B-29s on June 17. Each wing was assigned a different city: the 58th Wing went to Omuta, the 73rd to Hamamatsu, the 313th to Yokkaichi, and the 314th to Kagoshima. The targets were widely dispersed, separated by over 450 miles. Hamamatsu was on Honshu's Pacific coast east of Nagoya, Yokkaichi west of Nagoya on Ise Bay, Omuta in west-central Kyushu, and Kagoshima on Kyushu's southern coast.

That night's combined raids proved more successful in terms of urban area destroyed than most single-city maximum-effort incendiary raids. A total of over 6 square miles was burned by 456 B-29s dropping 3,058 tons of M-47 and M-69 incendiaries. Omuta lost almost a quarter of a square mile, Kagoshima more than 2 square miles, Hamamatsu just over 2 square miles, and Yokkaichi a little over 1 square mile. Japanese opposition was virtually nonexistent, their night fighters failing to catch the bombers heading towards the unexpected targets. These cities had almost no antiaircraft batteries; flak protection was negligible. One bomber was lost to "unknown causes."

The process was repeated on June 19–20 when 480 bombers struck Fukuoka, Toyahashi, and Shizuoka. Fukuoka was Japan's eighth-largest city; two wings went there. The 58th Wing went to Toyahashi and the 58th Wing to Shizuoka. Results mirrored those of the previous raid: minimal losses to the US bombers (two bombers were lost following a midair collision over Shizuoka), with major damage to the three cities hit.

A few days earlier, on June 16, Curtis LeMay was in Washington DC briefing Arnold on operations from the Marianas. The effectiveness of the campaign was then obvious. Arnold asked LeMay when the war would end. After consulting with one of his planners, LeMay came back and predicted the war would end by September 1, 1945. Based on the pace of operations, by that day all cities on the target list would have been burned, the Japanese transportation system would be bombed out, and the B-29s would have no more targets to bomb. LeMay was only off by a few days.

Compounding problems for Japan, the 315th Bombardment Wing flew its first operational mission on June 26. Its B-29s were equipped with AN/APQ-7 (Eagle) ground-tracking radar, designed for precision bombing rather than navigation. Its use required a 70-mile bomb run, so it was intended for high-altitude night bombing. Gun turrets were stripped from 315th Wing aircraft to increase bomb payload; an acceptable risk given Japan's weak night fighter capabilities.

While perfect for aerial mining, the 313th already had that job. LeMay made the 315th's primary task attacking Japan's oil industry. On June 26, one group bombed Utsube oil refinery at Yokkaichi, opening this campaign. It continued to the war's end. Sixteen missions were completed, most involving a group or two; two used the whole wing.

Bombing was accurate, with targeted refineries and storage facilities destroyed or heavily damaged by raids. Effectiveness suffered from the same problem as earlier raids against petroleum manufacturing and storage. Japan received too little crude oil to keep available refineries running, so most were idle and many tank farms were empty when hit.

The pattern was set for the rest of June, July,

A post-strike photograph of Oita, Japan, a town of 60,000 in northern Kyushu, after a July 16 incendiary raid. Twenty-five percent of the city burned, including the main business district (left and above arrow on the main business district street) which was almost completely destroyed. (AC)

and into August. During clear weather, planners scheduled precision daylight strikes against aircraft factories, arsenals, and industrial targets. When clouds were predicted, area raids against Japan's smaller cities were scheduled, with increasingly smaller cities being targeted. Meanwhile, the 315th Wing was destroying Japan's oil industry.

Except for a two-wing incendiary attack on Omuta on July 26, the maximum force sent against any individual target was one wing of bombers. Often precision raids involved only one or two bomb groups. Anywhere from 350 to 800 bombers might sortie, with up to eight different targets bombed on a single day.

Japanese opposition faded away. Japan's high command realized it could not stop the Superfortresses. It stopped trying, and Japan started husbanding what aircraft resources it had to resist what was viewed as the inevitable ground invasion. Thereafter, the main opposition the US bombers faced was antiaircraft artillery – of which there were too few guns to stem the incoming tide of aircraft.

Once the weakness of Japan's nighttime air defenses became obvious, LeMay had leaflets dropped the day before a raid urging civilians to leave. LeMay was not going to endanger his crews to safeguard Japan's civilians, but held no hostility against the civilian population. He just wanted to destroy Japan's industrial capability. Since Japan's military could not stop the night raids, leaflet warnings posed no threat. If it contributed to civilian demoralization, the warnings might even help shorten the war.

The daytime precision raids were successful when weather permitted visual bombing. After

Sea of Japan

PACIFIC OCEAN

East China Sea

Hokkaido

Honshu

Shikoku

Kyushu

Sado

IZU ISLANDS

OSUMI ISLANDS

KOSHIKIJIMA ISLANDS

City	1940 Population	% City Area Destroyed
Tokyo	6,778,804	51%
Osaka	3,252,340	35%
Nagoya	1,328,084	40%
Kyoto	1,089,726	n/a
Yokohama	968,091	58%
Kobe	967,234	56%
Hiroshima	343,968	40%
Fukuoka	323,400	22%
Kawasaki	300,777	35%
Kure	277,000	40%
Yawata	261,309	21%
Nagasaki	250,000	40%
Sendai	233,630	27%
Shizuoka	212,200	66%
Kumamoto	211,000	20%
Sasebo	206,000	48%
Shimonoseki	196,000	36%
Wakayama	195,260	53%

City	1940 Population	% City Area Destroyed
Kagoshima	190,250	44%
Sakai	182,150	44%
Omuta	177,000	42%
Amagasaki	175,000	19%
Gifu	172,340	74%
Hammamatsu	165,000	70%
Okayama	163,560	66%
Toyohashi	142,700	52%
Moji	139,000	27%
Kokura	130,000	n/a
Toyama	127,860	99%
Tokushima	119,600	74%
Nishinomiya	111,800	30%
Takamatsu	111,200	78%
Kochi	106,650	48%
Himeji	104,250	63%
Kofu	102,400	65%
Yokkaichi	102,000	60%

City	1940 Population	% City Area Destroyed
Ube	100,600	23%
Aomori	100,000	64%
Fukui	98,000	85%
Chiba	92,000	43%
Akashi	90,000	57%
Utsunomiya	87,868	34%
Maebashi	87,000	43%
Okazaki	84,070	68%
Hitachi	82,700	65%
Nobeoka	79,426	36%
Ichinomiya	70,800	75%
Tsu	68,625	57%
Shimizu	68,600	50%
Nagaoka	67,000	66%
Matsuyama	66,300	73%
Mito	66,300	65%
Miyazaki	65,000	26%
Hachioji	62,280	80%

City	1940 Population	% City Area Destroyed
Chosi	61,200	34%
Oita	61,000	25%
Imabari	60,000	76%
Miyakonojo	60,000	27%
Fukuyama	56,653	73%
Ogaki	56,100	40%
Numazu	53,165	90%
Ujiyamada	52,555	39%
Uwajima	52,100	50%
Saga	50,400	44%
Kumagaya	49,000	45%
Hiratsuka	42,150	44%
Kuwana	41,850	77%
Isezaki	40,000	17%
Tokuyama	38,400	37%
Tsuruga	31,350	68%
Omura	30,000	33%

Legend

- More than 50% city area destroyed
- 25–50% city area destroyed
- Less than 25% city area destroyed
- Railways
- Industrial belt

N

0 100 miles
0 100 km

Map city labels: Aomori, Sendai, Hitachi, Mito, Chosi, Chiba, Kawasaki, Yokohama, Tokyo, Hiratsuka, Utsunomiya, Isezaki, Numazu, Hachioji, Kofu, Kumagaya, Maebashi, Shimizu, Shizuoka, Hammamatsu, Nagaoka, Toyama, Fukui, Tsuruga, Gifu, Ichinomiya, Ogaki, Nagoya, Okazaki, Toyohashi, Kuwana, Yokkaichi, Tsu, Ujiyamada, Kyoto, Osaka, Sakai, Wakayama, Nishinomiya, Kobe, Himeji, Akashi, Amagasaki, Shodo, Awaji, Takamatsu, Tokushima, Okayama, Fukuyama, Hiroshima, Kure, Tokuyama, Imabari, Matsuyama, Kochi, Uwajima, Shimonoseki, Moji, Ube, Kokura, Yawata, Fukuoka, Saga, Oita, Omura, Kumamoto, Nobeoka, Miyazaki, Miyakonojo, Kagoshima, Iki, Sasebo, Nagasaki, Hirado, Nokadori, Goto, Tsushima

OPPOSITE RESULTS OF THE CAMPAIGN

All cities, except three which were atomic bomb targets (Hiroshima, Nagasaki, and Kokura) and one exempted from bombing for cultural reasons (Kyoto), were subject to incendiary raids.

June 16 only two more June days were suitable for daytime missions. Nearly 300 aircraft bombed aircraft factories and the Kure Naval Arsenal on June 22, then on June 26, over 450 B-29s attacked industrial targets throughout Honshu. The weather then closed in and the next daytime raids took place on July 24. That effort, coordinated with an Allied aircraft carrier strike against Kure, saw 625 B-29s leave the Marianas to strike seven different targets around Osaka and Nagoya.

While US and British carrier aircraft launched 1,747 sorties against targets in the Inland Sea, 573 B-29s dropped 3,539 tons of high explosives, destroying the Sumitoma Metal Company's propeller factory, Kawanishi's Takarazuka aircraft plant, Aichi's Eitoku aircraft factory, and Nakajima's assembly plant at Handa, while further damaging the Osaka arsenal.

Then the clouds rolled in again and there were no further daytime raids until August 7, a day after the first atomic bomb was dropped on Hiroshima. Neither that, nor the atomic bomb dropped on Nagasaki, stopped these raids. Three more days of major daytime raids were mounted between August 7 and the war's end on August 15. This included a 108-aircraft raid against the rail yards at Marifu, the opening of a campaign against the Japanese transportation network.

The incendiary raids followed a similar pattern. Between June 25 and August 14, 13 sets of night incendiary raids occurred. Each night saw at least 350 B-29s depart the Marianas. On each night four different Japanese cities were bombed. The next-to-last set of raids targeted Yawata, objective of the first bombing raid against the Home Islands. The results were markedly different this time. The 221 bombers reaching Yawata, burned out the city's heart. The smoke the next day was so thick that it obscured Kokura, the primary target for the second atomic bomb.

Hiroshima was Japan's seventh-largest city. On August 6, the city was flattened by a B-29 raid. One B-29, *Enola Gay*, attacked Hiroshima and dropped one bomb. The bomb was the Little Boy, with an explosive force of 15,000 tons of TNT – a payload which would have required 2,000 conventional B-29s to carry. It had been secretly developed by the Manhattan Project, the second-most expensive weapons development program of World War II, after the B-29.

The bomb was dropped by the 509th Composite Group, a unit which had flown solitary and secret missions since arriving on Tinian in April. By June the crews flying combat missions were mocking the men of the 509th because they seemingly avoided routine combat raids.

Even as it flew the first atomic mission, *Enola Gay* wore disguised markings. The aircraft carried the Circle-R of the 6th Bomb Group of the 313th Bombardment Wing, not a tail marking for the 509th. The 509th group had no unit identifier. On August 6, the whole world finally knew the secret. Forty percent of the city of Hiroshima was destroyed by this one bomb.

Three days later, *Bockscar* dropped a second nuclear bomb on Nagasaki. The bomb had to be dropped visually, and the sky was clear – or at least clear enough – to be dropped on the secondary target. Forty percent of Nagasaki, a smaller city than Hiroshima, was destroyed by a 21-kiloton plutonium bomb.

The two atomic bombs, or perhaps the declaration of war on Japan by the Soviet Union on August 7, provided Japan's government with a face-saving way to admit the inevitable and surrender.

AFTERMATH AND ANALYSIS

The B-29 *Sentimental Journey* flew 32 combat missions over Japan out of Guam, assigned to the 314th Bombardment Wing during this period. Retired to the Air Force's boneyard at Davis-Monthan AFB in 1959, in 1969 it was loaned to the Pima Air and Space Museum. Restored to its World War II appearance, it is now on permanent indoor display. (PASM)

The atomic bomb (along with the Soviet declaration of war) frequently gets credited for ending the war with Japan. But these events were less responsible for Japan's inability to continue the war than the combined effects of the mining and conventional strategic bombing campaign waged by the Twentieth Air Force and its subordinate XX Bomber Command and XXI Bomber Command.

Conventional bombing by these B-29s reduced 67 of Japan's largest cities to ashes, mostly through incendiary raids. Japan's factories and mills ground to a standstill through a lack of raw materials, and its population was starving, all due to the blockade imposed by naval mines dropped by B-29s. Two atomic bombs destroyed roughly 7 square miles in Hiroshima and Nagasaki. The firebombing campaign that began in March 1945 burned out 170 square miles of Japan's built-up urban area. The mining campaign reduced shipping by 98 percent.

Japan had been trying to find a way to end the war since June 1944, when the invasion of Saipan and the Yawata raid made clear that the Home Islands would soon be attacked. Because no one in the Japanese government wanted to admit Japan was defeated, the war continued for another 14 months. The two atomic bombs offered a justification for surrender. Japan's leaders could point to them as new weapons of immense power that were impossible to resist. Even after the two bombs fell, internal debate continued within the Japanese government.

After Nagasaki, the Allies suspended bombing, due to weather and political considerations, but Japan had still not agreed to surrender by August 12. Bombing was resumed on August 14, to make it clear Allied patience had limits. In addition to the raid on the Marifu rail yard, incendiary raids were made against Kumagaya and Isezaki. A 300-bomber daylight strike went after arsenals at Hikari and Osaka and a 315th Wing mission wiped out Japan's last operational oil refinery at Tsuchizaki. Of the 747 B-29s attacking that day not one was lost. It was a stunning display of US air power, the 1940s version of shock and awe.

The next day, Japan's war council, at the emperor's direction, agreed to surrender. That day, despite an attempted coup by mid-level Imperial Army officers, Japan laid down its arms. Emperor Hirohito broadcast an Imperial rescript stating "the war situation has developed not necessarily to Japan's advantage."

The formal surrender was signed on September 2, 1945 in Tokyo Bay, aboard the battleship *Missouri*, flagship of the Allied Pacific Fleet. As representatives of the Allied powers and the Imperial Japanese government signed the instrument of surrender, formations of Allied aircraft flew over the Allied fleet moored in Tokyo Bay. Among them was a formation of B-29s.

The B-29 soldiered on as a first-line US heavy bomber for five years. Because it was built as a war-emergency aircraft, it was not designed for long life. In 1947 it began to be replaced by the B-50, an aircraft that looked similar, but had a more robust framework and stronger, lighter skin. More importantly, it replaced the trouble-plagued Wright R-3350 with the 3,000hp, four-row, 28-cylinder Pratt & Whitney R-4360 Wasp Major radial engine. Both the B-29 and B-50 were replaced by the B-36 in 1949.

The Superfortress saw combat a final time during the Korean War. It was initially used as a daytime strategic bomber against North Korean cities, until MiG-15s appeared. After that it was a night bomber, interdicting supply lines. Some were converted to aerial tankers, weather aircraft, or similar auxiliary roles in the 1950s, but the last B-29 was retired from the USAF in 1961. In 1949 a Soviet version of the Superfortress appeared: the Tu-4 Bull was reverse-engineered from B-29s interned in Siberia during World War II. It was retired in the mid-1960s.

Curtis LeMay went on to be the first commander of the Strategic Air Command, eventually retiring in 1965 after serving as Air Force Chief of Staff from 1961 to 1965. For those services, which protected Japan from Communist invasion, Japan conferred the First Order of Merit with the Grand Cordon of the Order of the Rising Sun on LeMay in 1964, ironically presenting it on December 7, the anniversary of Japan's attack on Pearl Harbor. He dabbled in politics after retirement, running as vice-president on the third-party (and segregationist) American Independence Party in 1968. LeMay died on October 1, 1990.

The final conventional raids of the war were launched on August 14. They included a precision strike on the Marifu railyard, the opening attack on Japan's transportation system. The results are shown on this photograph. (LOC)

While the atomic bombs dropped on Hiroshima (shown here) and Nagasaki did tremendous damage and led Japan to surrender, they caused only a small fraction of the total destruction Japan experienced. Conventional bombardment was much more destructive. (LOC)

Japan's government was completely dismantled after its defeat, rebuilt as a parliamentary republic, with the emperor playing a largely ceremonial role. The military was abolished for nearly ten years, being reconstituted as the Japanese Self-Defense Force in 1954. Today the Japanese Army and Navy cooperate better than during the 1944–45 bombing campaign.

The strategic bombing of Japan proved unique. It was the first – and last – time one nation forced the surrender of a second nation through air power. Allied air superiority was a major contributor to Allied victory in Europe, but the Allied powers still needed to physically occupy the defeated Axis nations with ground troops before those nations surrendered. Those troops had to fight their way in against stiff opposition, albeit with the Allied troops aided by air power.

Similarly, air power alone won tremendous victories. The best example is the 1943–44 air campaign against Rabaul, which successfully neutralized Japan's biggest stronghold in the Southwest Pacific without requiring ground occupation of the bastion. Yet it never forced surrender of Japanese forces within the Gazelle Peninsula. That occurred in September 1945, when the garrison obeyed its Emperor's command to lay down its arms.

The atomic bomb offered Japan the excuse it needed to surrender before an invasion. Its War Council knew Japan was defeated. Allied forces had a base close enough to Japan to mount a ground invasion, while the B-29 bombing campaign had destroyed any meaningful ability to resist that invasion.

Without atomic bombs LeMay's planned offensive against Japan's transportation network might have forced surrender before November's D-Day for Operation *Olympic*, the invasion of Kyushu. Japan had already lost the food it imported from overseas. The collapse of its rail and road system would have prevented food moving from Japan's agricultural north to its industrial south. Starvation would doubtless have followed.

It is also possible that Japan might still have fought on, mobilizing its civilian population as a vast militia to resist the invasion. The resulting ground campaign would have left millions dead. The majority would have been Japanese, its ill-trained semi-civilian militias suffering the most casualties.

The success of the US bombing campaign against Japan convinced the upcoming generation of US air power advocates that air power alone could win wars. It had in Japan. Some believed that armies (and maybe navies) were obsolete. However, the United States' later wars demonstrated the necessity for ground troops. In Vietnam, the Gulf War, and the Iraq War, victory went to the nation putting boots on the ground in the decisive theater.

Whether conventional bombing would have led to Japan's surrender is debatable and irresolvable. What is beyond dispute is that the B-29s created conditions that made it impossible for Japan to repel an Allied invasion. The Twentieth Air Force and its subsidiary XXI Bomber Command destroyed Japan's industries, depriving the Imperial Japanese Army and Navy of the tools to resist invasion.

By August, Japan's industrial base was gone. Its aircraft industry was destroyed, its arsenals were in ruins, and its last oil refinery was smashed. Only the B-29s could have done this. The four-engine bombers used in Europe – the B-17, the B-24, and the Lancaster – lacked the range to reach much of Japan's industrial base. Even operating from bases in Okinawa, reaching targets in northern Kyushu and Shikoku would have been difficult. Nagoya and Tokyo were out of range. By contrast, B-29s with reduced bombloads could reach the northernmost places in Honshu, destroying the oil refinery at Tsuchizaki and fire-bombing Aomori.

Japan's aircraft production peaked in July 1944, shortly after the previous month's first tentative Superfortress raid against Yawata. By July 1945, monthly aircraft production had dropped 60 percent. A similar fall occurred in munitions production between March and July 1945. Ordnance output dropped only 18 percent between the peak production month of August 1944 and the start of March 1945, that largely due to import shortages.

The formal instrument of surrender was signed on September 2, 1945 on the deck of the Pacific Fleet's flagship, the battleship *Missouri*. A flyover of B-29s can be seen above the battleship. (USNHHC)

In 1940 Kyoto was Japan's fourth largest city. Kyoto was spared attack by both incendiaries and atomic bombs due to its cultural significance. It was largely undamaged at the war's end. (AC)

The effect of a firebombing raid is shown by comparing the prestrike reconnaissance photograph of Osaka's Minato district with the post-strike damage assessment photograph taken after the June 1, 1945 attack on the town. (AC)

By July 1945, due to strategic bombing, ordnance output dropped to only 40 percent of March's output. Shipbuilding dropped to only a quarter of the peak production between March and August. Electronics, chemicals, clothing, and other goods saw similar drops. Oil refining capacity was almost completely eliminated. Even if it had crude oil to refine, it had no plants in which to produce fuels.

The food situation was equally dire. Japan imported a fifth of its food in 1941. Even during peacetime Japan's food supply was barely adequate. Average caloric intake was then only 6.4 percent above bare subsistence levels.

Domestic food production plunged during the war years. The fishing fleet, which provided a significant fraction of Japan's domestic food production, was conscripted into the Imperial Navy or sunk by enemy action. Crop yields slumped as phosphates and nitrates used to fertilize fields were diverted to war production. Japan became more dependent on imported grains and beans from China and Korea, only to have its ports closed by B-29-dropped mines. Additionally, the incendiary campaign destroyed a quarter of Japan's food stockpiles between March and June 1945.

There was no question that the B-29 campaign was effective. But could Japan have stopped it? The answer is a qualified "maybe." There was nothing inevitable about US success.

The B-29 was appallingly ineffective during the first nine months of the strategic bombing campaign. Only one raid prior to the March 9–10 incendiary raid on Tokyo, the January 19 attack on the Kawasaki Aircraft Industries Company factory at Akashi, succeeded in destroying a target. That raid's success went unrecognized by XXI Bomber Command. By May 1945, precision bombing raids were hitting their targets, and by August most raids were so accurate that frequently only one trip per target was needed.

Many reasons for early failures existed. Crews lacked experience, especially with the B-29's electronics systems, including radar. Early versions of radar were optimized for navigation, not bombing accuracy. Bomb runs were made at too high an altitude, and the 500lb GP bomb proved too light to damage well-constructed factories.

Doctrinal changes and training solved most of these problems. The most important change in doctrine was LeMay's decision to switch from precision bombardment to area incendiary missions and to conduct the incendiary raids from low altitudes. This yielded a set of highly successful strikes in early March 1945. Subsequent precision raids later in March and early April failed to produce similar success.

The success of the March incendiary raids probably proved crucial to the continuation of strategic bombing using B-29s. The very-long-range and heavy-lift Superfortresses were

OPPOSITE
This postwar assessment of the July 1 incendiary raid on Ube shows how widely fires spread. Comparing it to the photograph taken earlier (page ?? image 59) during the raid shows how widely fires spread once local firefighters got saturated with more fires than they could handle. (AC)

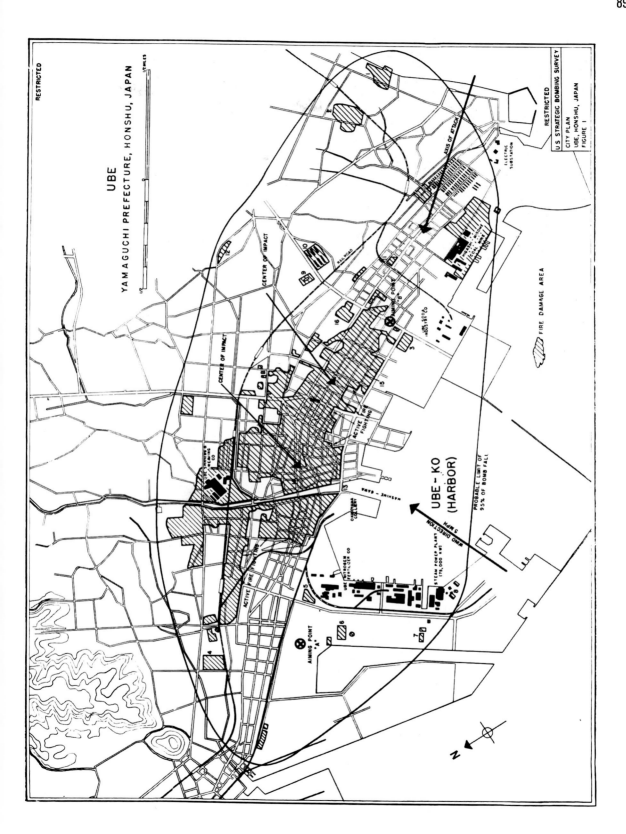

RESTRICTED

UBE
YAMAGUCHI PREFECTURE, HONSHU, JAPAN

UBE-KO (HARBOR)

RESTRICTED
U S STRATEGIC BOMBING SURVEY
CITY PLAN
UBE, HONSHU, JAPAN
FIGURE I

FIRE DAMAGE AREA

ELECTRIC POWER CONSUMPTION OSAKA

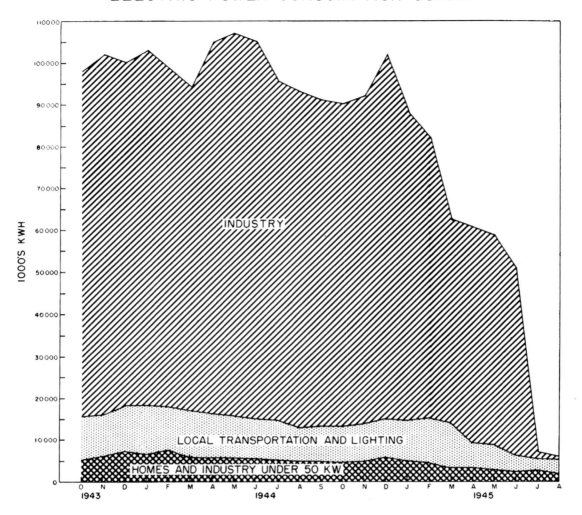

Industrial use of electricity in Osaka dropped from the 1944 highs between November 1944 and the March 1945 fire raid, due to supply shortages and dispersion of industry. It almost vanished after the June incendiary attacks. Virtually no industrial infrastructure remained to use electricity. (AC)

in demand outside the Twentieth Air Force and for missions other than strategic bombing. General George Kenney wanted them for Seventh Air Force long-range tactical support. The US Navy also wanted them as patrol aircraft or to run mining missions such as the ones done by the 313th Wing.

Patience with the B-29 strategic bombardment campaign was running out by January 1945. It was one reason LeMay replaced Hansell. In mid-April Nimitz was able to force Arnold to use the B-29s for a tactical mission – bombing the Kyushu airfields. It is possible that had strategic bombardment failed to produce any major success by mid-April, Arnold would have found the pressure to reduce or cancel the strategic bombardment campaign irresistible.

Reinforcements may then have been reassigned to other tasks, and the campaign wound down. Japan would still have lost the war, but the Allies would have invaded a Japan with its industrial capacity largely intact. A bloody land campaign against a much stronger Japanese Army would have occurred. Nuclear weapons would still have been used, but as tactical weapons to open Japanese lines for Allied forces to move through.

LeMay's decision to use low-level area raids showed courage on several levels. It contradicted Army Air Force doctrine. When incendiary attacks were suggested to Hansell he viewed it virtually as heresy, due to its wide divergence from accepted policy. LeMay decided to go low to get an optimum concentration of incendiaries. Others believed that decision foolhardy, as they did his decision to omit machine-gun ammunition to carry more bombs.

Yet LeMay read the situation correctly; his critics did not. Night raids against Japan, from the first Yawata raid on, revealed Japan's weakness in nighttime air defense. Japanese antiaircraft fire was inaccurate and night fighters ineffective. The concentrations LeMay demanded overwhelmed firefighters. Japanese industry was interspersed with residential areas, which were highly flammable, making fire-raids hellishly effective.

LeMay's tough decision gained a critical victory which bought time for XXI Bomber Command to find ways (other than fire raids) to bomb effectively. LeMay also found other innovative ways to use B-29s. These included his embrace of the aerial mining campaign advocated by Chester Nimitz (another heretical action according to many contemporary air power advocates), his willingness to experiment with precision nighttime bombing, and using 315th Wing for precision radar bombing.

The reason the Army Air Force had time to develop effective tactics was the impotency of Japan's home air defense. Japanese aircraft were unsuited for fighting the fast-flying, high-altitude, well-defended, and rugged B-29. Japan also assigned too few fighters to home defense. Japan then compounded these weaknesses.

It had an effective early warning system. Signal intelligence provided warning of days when B-29s would attack, picket ships provided long-distance warning, and its early warning radar network alerted Japanese interceptors. Yet Japan never integrated its air defense system. Its radar did not track incoming raids. It did not even advise fighters of the altitudes of incoming bombers. There was no set of plotting rooms to direct fighters: while the Royal Air Force and Luftwaffe achieved interception rates of 90–100 percent using such systems, Japanese pilots had to find the enemy on their own.

The Japanese Army and Navy failed to cooperate. Redundant air defense systems duplicated effort and wasted resources. The rival services failed to pass information between each other or coordinate attacks on incoming bombers. Both services compounded the problem by assigning fighters to geographic regions. Interceptors rarely found the enemy in a timely manner, and when they did they lacked the necessary strength to really punish bomber formations. Often, even before the bomber missions were escorted, bombers outnumbered the attacking Japanese fighters.

Had the Japanese built an integrated air defense, directing daytime fighters to the bombers at the same interception rates seen in Europe and vectoring interceptors from multiple services and sectors, the outcome might have been different. The US bombers would have been consistently met by several hundred fighters. If the first missions had resulted in loss rates equivalent to those seen in 1943 at Schweinfurt in Germany and other early, unescorted long-range European daytime missions, it is hard to see how the strategic bombardment experiment could have continued, especially given the ineffectiveness of early US bombing.

Similarly, while the neglect in building effective night fighters was almost criminal, those the Japanese did have could have been deployed more effectively by using an integrated air defense system. US night raids lasted 90 minutes to three hours, with aircraft entering the target area every 30 to 90 seconds. A squadron of night fighters, properly directed, could have had each aircraft find one Superfortress every five to ten minutes. Even with the radar tracking and jamming equipment carried aboard the B-29s, unacceptable bomber loss rates would have resulted.

Given sufficient Allied determination, Japan would still have lost. The cost would have been higher to both nations, as a ground invasion would have been required. Possibly a more vigorous air defense of Japan's Home Islands might have led to a negotiated end more in Japan's favor. Equally, it could have led to a Japan ravaged by atomic bombs. The

By the campaign's end, millions of Japanese were left homeless by the destruction of buildings in which they lived and worked. Many were reduced to preparing meals in a bucket in the ruins of what had been their homes. (AC)

Manhattan Project assembly lines were ready to ramp up production in September, and could have produced a bomb a week by spring 1946. Perhaps it was best that the Japanese air defense was so inept.

Surviving aircraft

Aircraft – from both sides – that fought in this campaign survive. It was the last aerial campaign of World War II. Any aircraft around that fought in it had no risk of being destroyed in future combat. Their remaining risk was that of any peacetime aircraft: accidental destruction or being scrapped. Even here the fates were kinder than they had been to aircraft from earlier in the war. The aircraft that fought over Japan were the latest models on both sides.

Of the nearly 4,000 B-29s built, 26 still exist. A 0.6 percent survivorship rate is impressive, considering the size and complexity of the aircraft. Of these, two are in flyable condition, 22 are static displays and two are in storage or under restoration.

Not all of these survivors are combat veterans of the strategic bombing campaign against Japan. At least nine did fly combat missions during World War II: three (including *Enola Gay* and *Bockscar*) belonged to the 509th Composite Group, while the other six flew conventional bombardment missions.

Except for *Enola Gay* and *Bockscar*, most were not preserved immediately after the war. Starting in the 1970s, several B-29s were rescued from places such as Naval Air Weapons Station China Lake and Aberdeen Proving Ground, where they had been sent to be expended on weapons testing. Instead they were restored and sent to museums in the United States and Great Britain.

Many more P-51s survive: there are over 250 examples including those requiring restoration. Of these, around 66 are on display in museums or at airbases in 18 different countries (although not at present in either Japan or Germany). Many others are privately owned and may be seen at airshows. Not all are of a type used in the strategic bombardment of Japan, and I could find no examples which I can confirm actually flew combat missions over Japan in support of B-29s.

Japanese aircraft are harder to find but some exist. There are five surviving examples of the Kawasaki *Hien*, although none seem to have seen service in Home Defense units. One Nakajima *Hayate* also survives. It was captured in the Philippines, so did not take part in defending the Home Islands. This aircraft is displayed at the Tokko Heiwa Kinen-kan Museum, Kagoshima Prefecture.

Four Kawanishi *Shiden* still exist. Of the three in the US, one is at the National Naval Aviation Museum in Pensacola, Florida, another is at the National Museum of the Air Force at Wright-Patterson AFB in Dayton, Ohio, and the third is at the National Air and Space Museum's Steven F. Udvar-Hazy Center. The one that is in Japan was recovered from the Bungo Strait. It was shot down during the campaign, so is a veteran of it. Partially restored, it is now displayed at Shinden-Kai Exhibition Hall (also known as Nanreku Misho Koen) in Uwajima on Shikoku Island.

Finally, one example each of a Kawasaki Ki-45 *Toryu* and Nakajima J1N1 *Gekko* also exist. Both are at the Steven F. Udvar-Hazy Center. The *Gekko* has been fully restored, but only the fuselage of the *Toryu* is on display.

FURTHER READING

There was a surprising amount of information about the strategic bombing campaign against Japan. It would not surprise me if it is the most-studied air campaign in history. One of the most informative popular accounts of the battle is *Superfortress*, written by Curtis LeMay and Bill Yenne. It has some of the weaknesses of a participant memoir (a tendency to overemphasize the author's contributions), but it was still an accurate treatment.

My preference is to use primary sources and official histories. Thanks to the internet, many sources which would have been difficult to locate 25 years ago are available digitally. Some make for dry reading or are highly technical, but I found them invaluable. Special notice should be taken of the numerous United States Strategic Bombing Survey reports. These attempted to measure the effectiveness of US bombing in a quantitative way. Most can be found at www.archive.org. All books with an asterisk following them can be found online.

The principal sources used for this book are:

Chilstrom, Maj John S., *Mines Away! The Significance of US Army Air Forces Minelaying in World War II*, Air University Press, Maxwell AFB, Alabama (1992)*

Craven, Wesley Frank, and Cate, James Lea (eds), *The Army Air Forces In World War II, Volume Five: The Pacific: Matterhorn to Nagasaki, June 1944 to August 1945*, Office of Air Force History, Washington DC (1983)*

Hansell, Haywood S., *The Strategic Air War Against Germany and Japan: A Memoir*, Office of Air Force History, United States Air Force, Washington DC (1986)*

LeMay, Curtis E., *Combat Crew Manual, XX Bomber Command*, APO 493 Saipan (December 1944)*

LeMay, Curtis E., and Yenne, Bill, *Superfortress: The Story of the B-29 and American Air Power*, Berkley Books, New York (1989)

Mason, Gerald A., Captain USN, *Operation Starvation*, Air War College, Air University, Maxwell AFB, Alabama (2002)*

Morrison, Wilbur H., *Point of No Return*, New York Times Books, New York (1979)

Price, Alfred, *Instruments of Darkness, The History of Electronic Warfare, 1939–1945*, Frontline Books, Barnsley, South Yorkshire (2017)

United States Strategic Bombing Survey, *Japanese Air Power*, Washington DC (1946)

United States Strategic Bombing Survey, *Effects of Incendiary Bomb Attacks on Japan: A Report on Eight Cities*, Washington DC (1947)*

United States Strategic Bombing Survey, *Effects of Air Attacks on Urban Complex Tokyo–Kawasaki–Yokohama*, Washington DC (1947)*

United States Strategic Bombing Survey, *The Effects of Air Attack on Japanese Urban Economy*, Washington DC (1947)*

United States Strategic Bombing Survey, *The Effects of Strategic Bombing on Japan's War Economy*, Washington DC (1947)*

United States Strategic Bombing Survey, *Effects of Air Attacks on the City of Nagoya*, Washington DC (1947)*

A *Shiden* displayed in the World War II Gallery at the National Museum of the US Air Force was one of three *Shidens* brought for evaluation to the United States after World War II. (NMUSAF)

United States Strategic Bombing Survey, *Effects of Air Attacks on Osaka–Kobe–Kyoto*, Washington DC (1947)*

United States Strategic Bombing Survey, *The War Against Japanese Transportation, 1941–1945*, Washington DC (1947)*

United States Strategic Bombing Survey, *The Japanese Aircraft Industry*, Washington DC (1947)*

United States Strategic Bombing Survey, *The Japanese Aircraft Industry*, Washington DC (1947)*

INDEX